KARATE-DO

KARATE-DO

by Tatsuo Suzuki 7th DAN

PELHAM BOOKS LIMITED

First published in Great Britain by
Pelham Books Limited
44 Bedford Square
London WC1B 3DLL
NOVEMBER 1967
SECOND IMPRESSION FEBRUARY 1975
THIRD IMPRESSION DECEMBER 1975
FOURTH IMPRESSION DECEMBER 1978
FIFTH IMPRESSION FEBRUARY 1982

Designed by M. Mohan

Drawings by Donald Green

ISBN 0 7207 0144 9

Printed in Great Britain by
Butler & Tanner Ltd, Frome and London

Contents

Prologue

Until recently I had not thought of writing a book on Karate, for it is my opinion that it is as difficult to express the elaborate techniques of Karate as those of any other sport, and also that it is not possible to acquire technique merely by reading books.

Since I settled in Britain, however, after travelling round the world, I began to feel a great desire to write about my experience. I wanted to convey the essence of Wadoryu (Wado school), in so far as I could, for Wadoryu was itself developed by rational study. It seems to me that of the many books on Karate hardly any explain and convey the real Karate. Furthermore, it seemed good to me to take the opportunity of writing my book here in Britain, since Karate has become increasingly popular all over the world, and English is such a widely known language.

I have put all that I have learned from my practice of Karate into this book. I have tried to analyse many techniques as far as possible, illustrating them by photographs taken from every angle.

The essential progress of a pupil in Karate is summed up in a Japanese saying, 'Obedience, divergence, and separation'. This means that first you must move correctly, as you are told by your instructor. Next, having mastered it, you must gradually break with this technique, so that subtly you develop your own style. Finally, you must separate yourself from your early practice, and your technique must follow naturally as a product of the blending of intention and movement.

However, the most important part is to have a good instructor in the basic techniques, for if you once learn bad techniques, it is very difficult to make any progress, and it takes time to correct bad technique even if later you go to a good instructor.

I am very fortunate in having had from the beginning of my practice, one of the best instructors, Mr. Hironori Otsuka.

It will be a great satisfaction to me if the publication of this book helps to spread true Karate.

Here I wish to record my appreciation to Mr. Menzies, of the magazine *Judo*, who took the photographs for this book in spite of the pressure of his business; to Mr. Wignall, Mr. Kono, Mr. Shiomitsu, Mr. Yamashita, Mr. Toyama; and to my good friends Mr. Resta, Mr. Beveridge, Miss Fong, and Miss Komiyama, who gave me great assistance in the preparation of the manuscript.

1 WHAT IS KARATE?

Karate is basically a training to bring a person back to the natural state of mind he was born with, dispelling delusions.

In *Fudochishinmyoroku*, a masterpiece in which the Zen master Takuan taught Yagyu Tajimanokami the essence of Kendo (Japanese fencing) through Zen Buddhism, a work highly valued by practitioners of Kendo and other forms of Budo (the martial arts), Takuan speaks of the real mind and the false or material mind as follows: The real mind is an inborn, pure mind, and the wordly mind is a mind soiled by evil thought and impressions through the experiences of life.'

Budo, he says, aims to restore this soiled, vicious mind to its natural state of purity, as it was at birth.

In the martial arts the aim is this: If our mind, as we make an attack, is attached to the idea of the opponent's counter-attack, we cannot fight with complete freedom, because we are not concentrating on our own actions, but are wondering if the opponent will kick against our punch, and so on. In the same way, while blocking we cannot counter-attack properly, with an empty mind, if we are preoccupied with the blocking itself, through fear of being knocked down by the opponent's kick or punch.

A baby does not have this complex of fear. A person who narrowly escapes being run over by a car will remain motionless, his limbs frozen by fear. But a baby would continue to move innocently, because he has no fear complex.

Someone once asked a famous Japanese fencing expert, 'What would you do if attacked suddenly?' 'When I am startled, I will step forward,' he replied. In a similar situation, an ordinary man would unconsciously step backward. This expert is able to act freely at any time and on any occasion, for he has an 'empty' mind, free from the illusions of life.

The essence of Budo, then, is to have a pure, empty mind, as at birth, free from doubts, fears, and delusions, according to the Zen master Takuan.

If our consciousness is too much attached to our action, that is, if our mind is attached to our punch while punching, or if it is obsessed only with the block while blocking, we cannot work freely.

Our ideas and thoughts ought not to be attached to anything. We ought not to allow our mind to become involved in anything. Seeing a flower, we admire its beauty. But if we wonder why this flower is so beautiful, or how long it has been in bloom, this means that we begin to have a mental attachment to the flower. Seeing a flower, or any other thing, only as it is and for its own sake, nothing of it remains in the mind. This is what is meant by a real, pure mind.

Similarly, an act, such as a punch or a block, ought to occur naturally, arising out of a pure or empty mind. This is one of the precepts of Zen.

It is said that the aim of Karate is to overcome oneself. It can be achieved only if one has this pure mind. If we are not attached to anything, we can accept everything. We must be free from attachments to the idea of hardship or pain in practice, for in this way we can bear this hardship or pain, and this means that we can overcome ourselves.

2 THE HISTORY OF KARATE

THE EARLY FORMS OF FIGHTING

Human combat is as old as human beings themselves. The first men, some 600,000 years ago, must have had to defend themselves against animals in the 'instinctive fight for survival'. But as man evolved and became different from the other animals, particularly in his mastery of language, fire, and tools, communities began to develop. It is possible that there was already fighting among men as early as this.

As the family emerged as the chief social unit, awareness of blood relationship would have led to feuds between clans.

Later, as agriculture developed, men began to keep domestic cattle, living in settled communities with more highly organized and complex structures. One class in this society which now grew up was the warrior-class, and men made for themselves weapons both for self-defence and for attacking enemies. This warrior-class, together with the religious class, the priests, formed the ruling element in human society.

In addition to the ancient practice of fighting between man and man, we find in many societies a highly sophisticated ritual, a branch of fighting, designed to represent the preservation or service of a god or gods. With the development of modified and improved weapons, elaborate rules of procedure for these rituals were formulated, and the foundations were laid of practices and techniques which still persist today.

The Art of Unarmed Combat

Europe

At the first Olympic Games (in 776 B.C.) there was an event called the *Pankration*. This was a form of all-in unarmed combat, and by the time Greece was overrun by the Romans, it had developed into the two modern sports of boxing and wrestling.

The techniques used in the *Pankration* included punching, kicking, throwing, and holding; but since the *Pankration* the art of unarmed combat in the West has been divided into two main streams. One of them, boxing, lays the chief emphasis on punching, the other, wrestling, on throwing and holding; the rules of each sport are formulated with these chief characteristics firmly in mind.

India

It is more than likely that the influence of these European techniques of fighting spread into Asia, following the invasion of Alexander the Great into India (336–323 B.C.). The Indian fist-arts also show some

Persian influence. The influence of some of these techniques, after they had been adopted in India, spread further throughout Asia in the wake of the Buddhist missionaries. Thus, for example, in Thailand, Thai-style boxing evolved, and in Java the fist-art called *penchac*.

China

The Indian martial art was introduced into China as one of the Buddhist practices, necessary in order to preserve health. T'ai Chi Chüan ('the fist-art of China') was developed by blending the Indian style with the ancient Chinese fist-art.

The founder of Zen Buddhism, Bodhi Dharma, being of royal blood, was instructed in the martial arts of India from his childhood.

Invited to China by the Emperor Wu of the Liang dynasty (about A.D. 520), he travelled there, where he undertook the form of meditation known as 'nine years facing the wall' at Shaolin-szu.

Having founded the Zen sect (A.D. 557) at the age of seventy-six, he taught his disciples the arts of the preservation of health, the eighteen ways of Lo-han, the *I-hu ching*, and the *Hsi-sui ching*, all of which had a marked influence on Chinese theories of fighting methods.

(a) *Kakuteijitsu* (*Chinese:* Chiao Ti Shu)
Chinese-style wrestling is called Chiao Ti Shu, or in Japanese, Kaku-teijitsu.

During the so-called 'Spring–Autumn period' (770–481 B.C.), and the period of civil wars (480–222 B.C.) the various arts of fighting, among which was the popular Kakuteijitsu, were highly valued among the noble classes in China.

During the Tsin (221–207 B.C.) and the Han dynasties (208–206 B.C.) the Chinese emperors, particularly Shia Huang Ti (the first Tsin Emperor) and the Han Emperor Liang Wu Ti patronized Kakuteijitsu, which soon spread among the military and the people, as a sport, with the result that techniques were gradually improved.

Kakuteijitsu in the Han period became known as Kaiko. In 1558 a Chinese named Ch'en Yuan Yün went over to Japan and lived at Shokokuji in Edo (now Tokyo), where he initiated the Japanese into the mysteries of Kakuteijitsu.

Today Kaiko is chiefly popular in Po Ting, in Ho Buk province, and it is known as Hotei (Po Ting) Kaiko (K'uai Chiao).

When the Mongols invaded China during the Yue period (1206–1368), they brought with them Mongolian wrestling, and this form of athletic art mingled with Kakuteijitsu and eventually became widespread.

During the Ming dynasty (1368–1644), however, people came to value technique and speed, and to despise mere physical strength, which the Mongols, on the other hand, emphasized.

(b) *Kenpo* (*fist-art*)
Originally Kenpo was called Kenyu or Gigeki ('art of attack'). At that time it was said: 'Gigeki is for the military class and Kakuteijitsu for the people.'

In ancient times, Gigeki was highly valued, and became extremely popular during the Han dynasty.

Gigeki was fairly similar to Kakuteijitsu in origin, and emphasized strength, but lacked the speed which was developed later, in Kenpo.

Kenpo probably developed from ancient Kakuteijitsu, just as boxing came from the *Pankration*.

Of all the fist-arts of China, Taikyokuken is the most popular today, and has also had an important effect upon the martial arts of Okinawa through China.

Taikyokuken has had such a considerable influence upon modern Karate that it is desirable to consider it here in more detail.

(c) *Taikyokuken* (*Chinese:* T'ai Chi Ch'üan)

Taikyokuken, founded at about the time of the end of the Ming dynasty and the beginning of the Chin dynasty, has a history of some three hundred years.

At that time there were a great number of fist-arts and methods of fighting developed in different schools all over China, all with their various merits and demerits.

During the Ming dynasty, the great general Ch'i Chi-Kuang (1528–1587), combined all the fist-arts of sixteen ancient and modern schools to produce his *Thirty-two zei of Kenkyo*, i.e. thirty-two fist positions, making them the basis of a standard style of fighting.

Half a century later, at the end of the Ming dynasty, General Ch'en Wang-T'ing, having studied and selected fist-arts from every school, perfected Taikyokuken, in which he adopted twenty-nine of Ch'i Chi-Kuang's Thirty-two zei.

Taikyokuken is the result of the union of the theories of fist-arts from many schools with ancient Tao-yin shu[1] and T'u-na shu[2] and in adaptation Ching-lo hsüeh-shuo,[3] which is a basic principle of Chinese medicine.

(d) *Modification of Taikyokuken*

Originally a fist-art, concerned with practical unarmed combat, Taikyokuken also contains elements for the preservation of health and fitness as well as the power of successful destruction in attack.

However, the development of firearms and other modern weapons about a century ago made fist fighting of less value in war, and consequently Taikyokuken has come to be used chiefly as an art for the preservation of health and fitness.

Today the most popular style of Taikyokuken is the Yo style, which Yang Lu-Ch'an (1799–1872) first introduced in Peking. Yang Lu-Ch'an and his second son, Pan Hou, taught it to Ch'i Jen, who initiated Wu Chien-Chuan (1870–1942), in mastery of this style.

Taikyokuken in Go style, is the second most popular style after the Yo style.

As Taikyokuken has many aspects and is very adaptable, anyone, man or woman, young or old, can practise it in any way, depending on the object he has in mind.

Not only does the present Chinese government recommend Taikyokuken as an important subject in the martial arts, but it is also used in medical treatment and physical education.

Okinawa

Karate (Empty Hand)

(a) *History*

Before the twelfth century little is known of the primitive community in Okinawa.

But in 1314 there is evidence that three powerful lords were in conflict. By 1429—more than a century later—the Lord of Nakayama Castle, Syo Hasshi, had united all the main islands by the sword.

This period corresponds to the Ming dynasty in China, and the Muromachi period in Japan.

---

[1] *Tao-yin shu:* physical exercises, consisting of bending and stretching, lying on one's back or front.

[2] *T'u-na shu:* art of abdominal breathing. Both Tao-yin shu and T'u-na shu are ancient Chinese arts for the preservation of health.

[3] *Ching-lo hsüeh-shuo:* the theory of exercising the internal organs to promote free circulation of the blood.

Synthesizing these elements: fist-arts, the techniques of preserving health and of breathing, backed by medical theory, Taikyokuken unites control of consciousness, breathing, and movement in practice.

Throughout the course of this period there was extensive trade with China, and in 1392 Chinese immigrants were permitted to settle.

Relations with Japan were also active.

It was during this period that the Japanese pirate Wako infested the seas around Okinawa.

Although the martial arts of Japan and China influenced those of Okinawa, they were not very popular, as there had been peace under the thriving Buddhist culture since the political union of the islands by Syo Hasshi.

In 1609, the islands of Ryukyu were easily conquered by troops despatched by the Satsuma clan in Japan.

The prince of Okinawa was taken as a hostage and a police force was established at Naha (the capital of Okinawa) to superintend internal affairs.

The military class was banned and all arms were confiscated. For this reason the combative techniques of Okinawa, which have been handed down to the present day, use only the stick, the club, and Karate—the empty hand.

(b) *The Name Karate*

Karate was originally called 'Tode' (T'ang hand) or just 'Te' (hand) in Okinawa.

It is recorded that a certain Karate instructor in Okinawa, Nagashige Hanagusuku, used the Japanese characters Karate (Empty hand) instead of T'ang in August 1905.

In Japan, the instructor Gichin Funakoshi changed T'ang hand to Karate (Empty hand) about 1930.

Now, the Japanese character 'Kara' (or Ku) symbolizes the essence of Budo (martial way), which is to defend oneself against an enemy with empty hands.

Those who practise this form of unarmed combat should always empty their minds, clearing them of selfish and evil thoughts, as 'an empty valley conveying sound'. It is said in Buddhism : 'Form is emptiness. Emptiness is form.' If one observes the phenomena of the universe, everything is empty. Emptiness is indeed the truth of everything.

Although there are various Oriental martial arts, such as jujitsu, fighting with sword or spear, archery, or duelling with cudgels, the basis of them all is the same as that of Karate : Karate is the most basic of all the martial arts, for it teaches fighting with no more weapons than a man is born with, and follows the teaching of emptiness as in Zen Buddhism.

(c) *Schools of Karate*

(1) Shito school (founder Kenwa Mabuni)

The name of this school comes from Japanese characters of instructors Itosu and Higaonna. It is popular chiefly in the west of Japan.

(2) Goju school (founder Chojun Miyagusuku)

This derives from the same origin as the Shito school. The name is taken from the Japanese words *Goken* (strong fist) and *Juken* (soft fist). It is also popular in the west of Japan.

(3) Shotokan school (founder Gichin Funakoshi)

Named after the term Funakoshi used for calligraphy : Shoto. Prevailing mainly in the east of Japan.

(4) Wado school (instructor Hironori Otsuka)

Called Wado (way of peace) in the belief that the basis of Budo (martial way) is the way of peace. Also popular in the east of Japan.

(d) *Introduction of Karate*

1912 : Ten officers of Japan's First Fleet had training in Karate for one week in Okinawa.

1920 : Norimichi Yabe (instructor in Karate of the Okinawa Teacher's College) gave a demonstration of Karate in Los Angeles, U.S.A.

1921 : Instructor Gichin Funakoshi introduced Karate in Tokyo.

1923 : Asamoto Motobu introduced Karate into Osaka (Japan).

Japan

(a) *Sumo*

Although it has been claimed that Sumo is derived from the Chinese Kakuteijitsu, it seems probable to me that Sumo started in Japan and developed from the ancient type of defensive combat like the other arts of fighting.

It is evident that Sumo was originally a form of combat with no holds barred, fought until one opponent knocked down the other, like the Chinese Kakuteijitsu and Greek *Pankration*.

For example, it is recorded that in the Yamato period, Nomino Sukune and Taimano Kehaya wrestled in the presence of the Emperor Suinin, and Sukune broke one of Kehaya's ribs and his hip-bone by kicking, and then stamped him to death.

However, such techniques as punching, striking, and kicking were forbidden during the Naro period. Sumo has become a sport rather than a martial art in earnest. Today, Sumo is a Japanese national sport, and is very popular among both professionals and amateurs.

(b) *Jujitsu*

As fighting in the Genpei and the Kamakura periods usually took the form of single combat in heavy armour, the popularity of wrestling increased greatly.

But since the Strife of Onin (1469), in the Nanboku period, light armour took the place of the heavy type.

In the following Sengoku period (civil war period), Takeuchi Minamoto Hisamori founded the Takeuchi school of Jujitsu (1532). He systematized all the known techniques of unarmed fighting, selecting them from the martial arts of his time, and developing them in his own style. It could be claimed that thus Jujitsu was to some extent influenced by Sumo.

After the Takeuchi school of Jujitsu was founded, many other schools followed. Jujitsu in those days was a kind of wrestling, designed as practice for fighting in earnest on the battlefield.

In 1558, at the end of the Ming dynasty, the Chinese Ch'en Yuan Yün came over to Japan and instructed Fukuno Masakatsu, Miura Yoshitatsu, and Isokai Jirozaemon in Kakuteijitsu, Kinshoho, and fighting with the arms (similar to jiujutsu).

Fukuno developed Shintoryu Wajitsu, and his pupil Ibaragi Mataemon founded Kitoyu.

About that time, Akiyama Shirobē of Nagasaki went to China to study medicine, and there he was initiated into the mysteries of Byakuda sante (one of the Chinese fist-arts) and Kappo in 28 Ryu (twenty-eight ways of reviving) by a Chinese military officer, and on his return he founded Yoshinryu.

The honourable instructor Hironori Otsuka, who is the highest authority on Japanese Karate, and also the founder of Wadoryu, practised Shintoyoshinryu (a development of Yoshinryu) from his childhood, and became thoroughly conversant with it. He adopted the best points of the original Japanese Jujitsu and blended them with Okinawa Karate.

Summary.

It is apparent that Karate was most influenced by the Chinese fist-art, although the origin of Karate can be traced back to *Pankration* in Europe.

When Okinawa began to pay tribute to the Ming emperors, the Chinese fist-arts, developed by Ch'i Chi-Kuang and Ch'en Wang-Ting were introduced into Okinawa. As time went by, they were blended with the original native martial arts.

But later, due to the ban on weapons of Satsuma, the unique Okinawa Karate, that is the art of developing the hands and feet as lethal weapons, was evolved, and spread throughout the island.

This Karate was introduced into the mainland of Japan in 1921, took over a few good points from Japanese Jujitsu and this has developed in Japan as Nihon Karate-do today.

There is some similarity between the Chinese fist-arts and Karate, although the primary purpose of present-day Chinese fist-arts is physical training and the preservation of health. Japanese Karate, on the other hand, following Okinawa Karate, was developed as a martial, lethal art for practical fighting, although it, too, has become a sport today. There is a great difference of approach and attitude in that the Japanese Budo spirit (spirit of the martial way) is put into it.

It is worth mentioning here that on the occasion of the Tokyo Olympic Games in 1964, Japanese Karate, which had been divided into many schools, formed a federation, the All-Japan Karate Association, sponsored by the Ministry of Education, in October of that year.

It is possible that Karate-do will join the Japan Athletic Association, and thus there will be a valid All-Japan Championship and there may also be in the future a Karate event in the Olympic Games. It gives me great satisfaction that Karate-do is now becoming more and more popular all over the world.

3 METHODS OF ATTACKING VITAL POINTS

See Diagram 1

Centre of the Skull
Bottom fist—elbow

Temples
Fore fist, back fist—ridgehand—elbow—knifehand—middle finger—one knuckle fist—instep (roundhouse kick)

Bridge of Nose
Hand: Fore fist—back fist—knifehand—middle finger—one knuckle fist—ridgehand—forehead

Under the Nose
Hand: Fore fist—back fist—middle finger—one knuckle fist—ridgehand—forehead
Foot: Knee—foot edge

Side of Chin
Hand: Palm heel—fore fist—elbow
Foot: Instep (roundhouse kick)

Front of Chin
Hand: Fore fist—palm heel
Foot: Ball of foot (front kick)—knee—foot edge—heel (back kick)

Adams Apple
Hand: Middle finger—one knuckle fist—one finger spearhand—knifehand—ridgehand

Side of Neck
Hand: Knifehand—bottom fist—ridgehand
Foot: Instep (roundhouse kick)

Pit of Neck
Hand: Two finger spearhand

Armpit
Hand: Middle finger—one knuckle fist—elbow

Heart
Hand: Fore fist—backhand—back fist—palm heel—elbow—ridgehand
Foot: Ball of foot—foot edge—instep (roundhouse kick)—knee—heel (back kick)

Solar Plexus
Hand: Fore fist—back fist—middle finger—one knuckle fist—four finger spearhand—ridgehand—palm heel—elbow
Foot: Ball of foot (both)—knee—heel (back kick)—foot edge

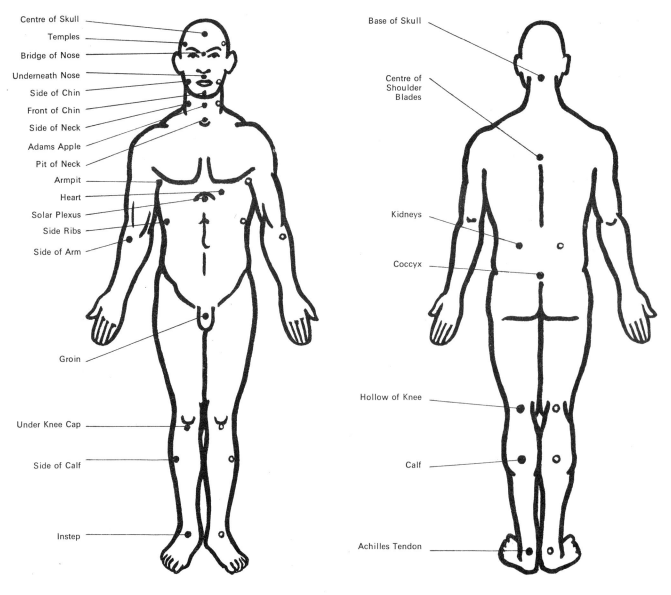

Centre of Skull
Temples
Bridge of Nose
Underneath Nose
Side of Chin
Front of Chin
Side of Neck
Adams Apple
Pit of Neck
Armpit
Heart
Solar Plexus
Side Ribs
Side of Arm

Groin

Under Knee Cap

Side of Calf

Instep

Base of Skull

Centre of
Shoulder
Blades

Kidneys

Coccyx

Hollow of Knee

Calf

Achilles Tendon

Diag. 1   **The vital points of the body**

Side Ribs
Hand: Fore fist—middle finger—one knuckle fist—elbow—palm heel
Foot: Ball of foot (front kick)—foot edge

Side of Arm
Hand: Knifehand—bottom fist

Groin
Hand: Ridgehand—back fist—fore fist—palm heel
Foot: Ball of foot (front kick and roundhouse kick)—instep (roundhouse kick)—knee—heel (back kick)

Under Knee Cap
Foot: Foot edge—ball of foot (front kick)

Side of Calf
Foot: Ball of foot—foot edge—heel (back kick)

Instep
Foot: Heel (back kick)

Base of Skull
Hand: Knifehand—bottom fist—middle finger—one knuckle fist—elbow
Foot: Instep (roundhouse kick)

Centre of Shoulder Blades
Hand: Fore fist—middle finger—one knuckle fist—bottom fist—elbow
Foot: Ball of foot (front kick and roundhouse kick)

Kidneys
Hand: Middle finger—one knuckle fist—bottom fist—palm heel—elbow—fore fist
Foot: Ball of foot (front kick and roundhouse kick)—knee

Coccyx
Foot: Ball of foot (both)—knee

Hollow of the Knee
Foot: Ball of foot (both)—foot edge

Calf
Foot: Ball of foot (both)

Achilles Tendon
Foot: Foot edge—heel—ball of foot

PREPARATORY EXERCISES

Special preparatory exercises, light gymnastics, and other training methods to strengthen hands and feet, are important in Karate.

To perform the techniques of Karate we need these special training methods since we bring into play muscles which are not used in other sports. If you practise these preparatory exercises and light gymnastics before you practise the various Karate techniques, you will master the techniques more readily and more effectively.

You can adapt preparatory exercises from other sports, but here are some special ones for Karate, shown in photographs on pages 21–24.

Relaxing and Stretching Exercises

These exercises are very important because the beginner must stretch his leg and make the muscles soft and supple in order that when he kicks high it will prove easy and he will not lose his balance. These exercises must be done at the beginning of each training session.

See Figs. 1, 2a, 2b.
In this exercise it is important to keep the instep straight so that the leg

and instep are in line; also keep the toes back in the same way as the front kick. The knee must not be bent. Begin with the back straight, then bend forward to touch the knee with the forehead. Fig. 2 is very difficult for beginners. They can hold on to their partner's jacket or put their hands round his neck until their legs are stretched sufficiently to do without any support. These two exercises are done with the left and right leg— twenty times each.

See Figs. 3a, 3b, 4a, 4b.
These exercises are for stretching the leg for the foot-edge kick (sokuto). Kick the leg sideways and lift up from the sides and not the front. As this sokuto kick is delivered by the edge of the foot near the heel, in this exercise the foot must be kept well turned with the heel upwards. When the body is bent to touch the knee with the forehead, it is twisted round to the front at the waist. The person holding the foot must turn the front of the foot down and outwards, Fig. 3b. This also must be done with both left and right leg, twenty times each.

See Figs. 5a, 5b.
Keep the leg straight and touch the knees with the forehead.

See Figs. 6a, 6b.
The leg must be open as wide as possible. Touch the floor with the forehead.

See Figs. 7a, 7b.
Twist the waist to the left and to the right.

See Figs. 8a, 8b, 8c.
Pull the feet right into the body, bend forward and touch the floor with the forehead.

See Figs. 9a, 9b.
After doing this exercise to the right, change legs and do it to the left. All these exercises should be done ten or fifteen times each. If the beginner finds these exercises difficult to do, then someone can stand behind and help by pushing the body down.

See Figs. 10, 11, and 12.
The knees must not be bent. First practise with the left leg then the right leg. Each time kick as high as possible. Each exercise ten times for both left and right leg.

See Fig. 13.
In this exercise the top man must relax and allow his legs to hang down. Then reverse positions so that the man at the bottom becomes the man at the top. Keep changing positions about ten or fifteen times.

Strengthening Exercises

See Figs. 14a, 14b.
First the big toes up and the small toes pressed down, then change with big toes pressed down and small toes lifted up.

See Figs. 15a, 15b.
First turn the feet and stand on the outside edge, then turn the knees inwards and twist the feet on to the inside edge.

See Figs. 16a, 16b, 16c.
First arc the body forwards, bend the knees and raise the heels. Then snap the knees straight and lift the toes, bending the body forwards slightly from the waist. This exercise is for balance and strengthening the knees. All these exercises are to be done about twenty times each.

See Figs. 17a, 17b, 17c.
From hanmi gamae put the leg out straight—the same as for front kick.

continued on page 25

Fig. 1

Fig. 2a

Fig. 2b

Fig. 3a

Fig. 3b

Fig. 4a

Fig. 4b

Fig. 5a

Fig. 5b

Fig. 6a

Fig. 6b

Fig. 7a

Fig. 7b

Fig. 8a

Fig. 8b

Fig. 8c

Fig. 9a

Fig. 9b

Fig. 10

Fig. 11

Fig. 12

Fig. 13

Fig. 14a

Fig. 14b

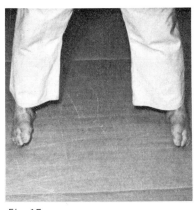

Fig. 15a

Fig. 15b

Fig. 16a

Fig. 16b

Fig. 16c

Fig. 17a

Fig. 17b

Fig. 17c

Fig. 18a

Fig. 18b

Fig. 19a

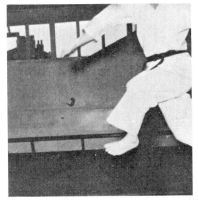

Fig. 19b

Fig. 20a

Fig. 20b

Fig. 21a

Fig. 21b

Fig. 21c

Fig. 22a

Fig. 22b

Fig. 22c

Fig. 22d

Fig. 23a

Fig. 23b

Fig. 23c

Then bend the supporting leg to Fig. 17c. Next, straighten the supporting leg and pull the other leg back to the starting position.

Exercises for Fast Jumping

See Figs. 18a, 18b.
Draw two parallel lines about one metre twenty centimetres (3 ft. 11¼ in.) apart. Then, keeping the feet outside the lines, jump from side to side, first moving forwards then backwards. It is important to straighten the knees at each jump and jump as high and far sideways as possible each time. Do not pause between each jump, but jump as quickly and as rhythmically as possible.

See Figs. 19a, 19b.
Cross the legs so that when jumping to the right the left foot is the landing foot, and when jumping to the left the right foot is the landing foot.

See Figs. 20a, 20b.
This is called Rabbit Jumping. This exercise is more effective if practised up and down stairs. Keep the back straight.

For Strengthening the Hips

See Figs. 21a, 21b, 21c.
Stand with the feet slightly wider apart than the shoulders and turn the toes inwards slightly, bend the knees and keep the hips low. This is called Kibadachi. Keep the back straight. Cross the feet over in front, keeping the Kibadachi stance. Move to the left several places, then back to the right, then again to the left, etc. It is important to keep in correct Kibadachi stance all the time. Then from the Kibadachi stance quickly lift the left leg inward and touch the knee with the bottom of the foot. Repeat with the right foot to the left knee.

Fist, Wrist, and Arm Strengthening Exercises

See Figs. 22a, 22b.
This exercise should be done on a hard floor. A soft floor or mat is no use. Only the two striking knuckles touch the floor. About thirty times up and down is sufficient.

See Fig. 22c.
Bend the arms and lift alternate legs. Do not bend the knees.

See Fig. 22d.
With the arms straight, walk forward on the fist, dragging the feet.

Makiwara Exercises

Makiwara training is very important for correct punching techniques, with particular emphasis of fore-fist punching. The object of Makiwara training is to strengthen the hips and the wrists. Just arm punching is very bad. *See Figs. 23a and 23b.*

Note 1. The hips must be twisted sideways with the body weight on the back leg which is bent, the body leaning backwards slightly. Now the hips are twisted quickly to the front and the back foot is turned to face the front, twisting on the ball of the foot. Straighten the back leg and bend the front leg. Transfer all the weight to the front foot.

Note 2. Keep the heel of the back foot on the floor. The elbow of the punching arm must be kept down. *See Fig. 23c.*

Note 3. Shoulders must be relaxed all the time.

Note 4. Keep the eyes on the target all the time.

Note 5. Pull back the other hand quickly to the hip.

continued on page 28

Fig. 23d

Fig. 24a

Fig. 24b

Fig. 25a

Fig. 25b

Fig. 26a

Fig. 26b

Fig. 27a

Fig. 27b

Fig. 28a

Fig. 28b

Fig. 28c

Fig. 28d

Fig. 29a

Fig. 29b

Fig. 29c

Fig. 29d

Fig. 30

Fig. 31a

Fig. 31b

See Fig. 23d.
This is the same technique as before but strike with the elbow.

See Figs. 24a, 24b.
This technique is for Uraken (back fist). The stance is to the side of the Makiwara. The twisting of the hips and moving the body weight is the same as for the previous technique.

See Figs. 25a, 25b.
This technique is the same as Uraken punching.

See Figs. 26a, 26b.
This technique is Haito or ridgehand. The leg position is the same as Uraken, but the arm is kept straight and the punch is a swing.

Iron Shoes Exercises

Beginners must be careful not to overdo these exercises at first or they will injure the knee joint. The iron shoes must be secured to the foot by a judo belt or there is a danger of them flying off the foot during a kick. Before starting to kick, a little limbering up, by walking or running in the iron shoes, is advised.

See Figs. 27a, 27b.
Keep the legs straight and lift the foot high.

See Figs. 28a, 28b, 28c, 28d, 29a, 29b, 29c, 29d.
Beginners must do these exercises twenty times each leg. Advanced students thirty or forty times.

See Fig. 30.
This is a photograph of Makiwara training and iron-shoes kicking in Japan.

Training with the Lighted Candle

See Figs. 31a, 31b.
This is training for shoulder relaxing, speedy punching, and wrist twisting, and also a strong snap finish. At first, stop about four centimetres (1½ in.) from the flame, then if the candle goes out every time, stop about six centimetres (2½ in.) away. As you become more proficient move further away. A punch that can put out the candle at about twenty centimetres (7¾ in.) is considered very good. It is not necessary to practise putting out the candle with shuto or kicking.

4 HOW TO USE THE HANDS & FEET IN KARATE

Diag. 2 Fore fist

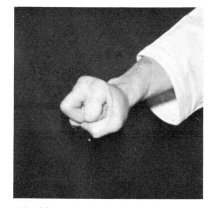

Fig. 32

Hand

(1) *Seiken* (*Fore Fist*)
See Fig. 32. Diagram 2.

The striking point is the shaded area, particularly the middle knuckle. The fingers must be tightly rolled excluding all the air. The thumb must be placed across the finger pressing on the middle one. The little finger must be kept tight at all times. Of all the hand techniques, the seiken is the most used. Makiwara training is very important in developing a strong seiken.

(2) *Nakadakaipponken* (*Middle Finger—One Knuckle Fist*)
See Fig. 33.

Make a fore fist, then push out the middle finger and place the thumb on the first joint of the middle finger and strike with the second joint. This punch is used to strike the solar plexus, lower ribs, and in the armpit. If the face is struck, the twisting of the punch can tear the flesh.

(3) *Haito* (*Ridgehand*)
See Fig. 34.

Bend the first finger and push the first joint in with the thumb. Attack can be made on the opponent's nose by striking upwards with the second joint of the bent first finger, and effective attack can also be made by using the area of the first finger and thumb to attack the neck, stomach, or the groin.

(4) *Tetsui* (*Bottom Fist*)
See Fig. 35.

Make a fore fist, with the soft part between the little finger knuckle and the wrist bone as the striking area.

(5) *Shuto* (*Knifehand*)
See Fig. 36.

The striking area is the same as the bottom fist, but the hand is open. Both tetsui and shuto are very good striking techniques, but care must be taken not to strike with the little finger knuckle or the wrist bone—or injury may occur. These techniques are very good for attacking the throat, the back of the neck, or collar bone. Sometimes these techniques are open to counter-attack by the fore fist, because they are usually delivered in a circular manner while the fore fist is a straight punch.

(6) *Uraken* (*Back Fist*)
See Diagram 3.

Strike with the back of the knuckles, sometimes with the hand clenched and also with the hand open. This is a good technique because it can be delivered very fast.

Fig. 33

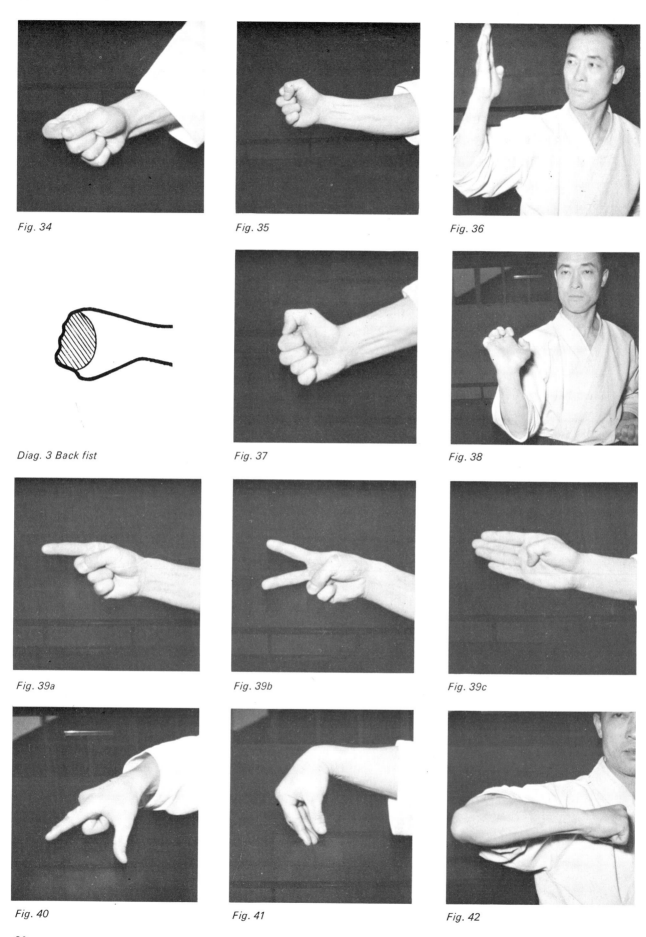

Fig. 34

Fig. 35

Fig. 36

Diag. 3 Back fist

Fig. 37

Fig. 38

Fig. 39a

Fig. 39b

Fig. 39c

Fig. 40

Fig. 41

Fig. 42

(7) *Hiraken (Middle Finger—Four Knuckle Fist)*
See Fig. 37.

This is the same as seiken, but, with the thumb on the side of the first finger, strike with the middle joint of the finger. This is used for blocking an attack by kick or punch. The block is made with a quick wrist movement.

(8) *Teisho (Palm Heel)*
See Fig. 38.

The fingers and thumb are pressed tightly in, and the striking area is the lower part of the palm of the hand. This is used to strike underneath the chin or the ribs, or the solar plexus with an upward movement. It is also used as a block against a punch or kick.

(9) *Nukite (Spearhand)*
See Figs. 39a, 39b, 39c.

This technique can be used with one, two, or all the fingers. One finger spearhand is used to attack the pit of the neck and the stomach. Two finger spearhand is used to attack the eye, and four finger spearhand is used to attack the eyes and stomach. This technique is very dangerous and cannot be used in free fighting or contest.

(10) *Hirabasami (Clawhand)*
See Fig. 40.

This technique is used to attack the neck. The finger and thumb are closed round the neck, gripping as hard as possible, while the first knuckle of the second finger is pushed forward.

(11) *Kakuto (Bent Wrist)*
See Fig. 41.

This is a block with the back of the wrist, which is bent.

(12) *Hiji (Elbow)*
See Fig. 42.

This is a very strong attacking technique, especially suitable for women to use. It can be used as a roundhouse strike, or upwards, sideways, and downwards strike.

Foot Technique

(1) *Jōsokutei (Ball of the Foot)*
See Fig. 43.

The toes must be kept back, and the striking area is the ball of the foot. This is used in the front kick and roundhouse kick.

(2) *Ashikubi (Instep)*
See Fig. 43.

The striking area is the instep. One kind of roundhouse kick uses the ball of the foot and the other uses the instep to attack.

(3) *Hiza (Knee)*
See Fig. 44.

The striking area is the knee.

(4) *Sokuto (Foot Edge)*
See Fig. 45.

This is used with the side kick.

(5) *Kakato (Heel)*
See Fig. 46.

Strike with the centre of the heel. This is used with the back kick and also the stamping kick.

Fig. 43

Fig. 44

Fig. 45

Fig. 46

Basic Techniques for Kicks

(1) *Maegeri* (*Front Kick*)
Please refer to basic technique for punch and kick.

(2) *Sokuto* (*Foot Edge Side Kick*)
See Figs. 47a–g.
This kick is used to attack the knee, the middle of the body, and the face. First, facing front, lift the knee, keeping the toes up; then twist the hips and kick at the same time.

Note 1. Relax the body and snap the kick as quickly as possible.

Note 2. Good timing is very important, as is correct distance. If both timing and distance are bad the kick becomes a push with no power.

Note 3. The foot must be twisted so that the front of the foot is pointing downwards with the toes back. Strike with the edge of the foot below the ankle. If the striking is done with the edge of the foot near the little toe, there is no strength in the kick and damage may occur to the foot.

Note 4. These photographs are mainly for beginners. After proficiency is reached, the kick can be delivered to the side and upwards at once. This makes the kick much quicker and it can be used to good effect in free fighting and contest.

(3) *Mawashigeri* (*Roundhouse Kick*)
See Figs. 48a–f.

These photographs show one step leading into a roundhouse kick, but there are other ways of kicking: Kicking with the rear foot without moving forward, and also a roundhouse kick with the front foot. Roundhouse kicks to the face and groin are usually delivered with the instep, but for kicking to the stomach the ball of the foot is stronger. The instep can be used to attack the stomach also. This is a speedier kick and straighter than kicking with the ball of the foot. It is also easier.

Note 1. Face the front, then kick by twisting the hips and raising the knee.

Note 2. Do not take the foot in too wide a circle.

Note 3. Snap the kick.

Note 4. After the kick, make sure to maintain a good balance.

(4) *Ushirogeri* (*Back Kick*)
See Figs. 49a, 49b, 49c.
Bend the foot inwards so that the strike can be made with the heel.

Note 1. Lift the knee and pull the foot up to the body. Fig. 49d is incorrect.

Note 2. When kicking keep the leg and body straight.

Note 3. The face must be kept forward and not turned round to watch an opponent as this makes the kick go sideways and weakens it. Fig. 49e is incorrect.

Note 4. After kicking, the body must be quickly straightened and twisted to the front—maintaining a good balance.

(5) *Uraken* (*Back Fist*)
See Figs. 50a–d.

1. *See Fig. 50a.* The body must face the front.

2. *See Figs. 50b, 50c.* First the right arm moves across the body with the back of the hand facing outwards, then the hips are twisted to the left. At the same time the fist comes up to the opponent's face and delivers a punch with the back of the fist. The left arm is raised to a defensive position by the chest—but not touching it.

continued on page 36

Fig. 47a

Fig. 47b

Fig. 47c

Fig. 47d

Fig. 47e

Fig. 47f

Fig. 47g

Fig. 48a

Fig. 48b

Fig. 48c

Fig. 48d

Fig. 48e

Fig. 48f

Fig. 49a

Fig. 49b

Fig. 49c

Fig. 49d

Fig. 49e

Fig. 50a

Fig. 50b

Fig. 50c   *Fig. 50d*

3. *See Fig. 50d.*

After the punch the arm is relaxed and quickly pulled back. The body is still kept sideways.

Note 1. It is very important to snap the wrist during the punch.

Note 2. The body must lean forward during the punch.

Note 3. The eyes must be kept on the opponent all the time.

5 THE BASIC PUNCH & KICK

1. Foundations of Karate Technique

As the basic punch and kick are the foundations of all Karate techniques, it is impossible to make progress in the more advanced techniques without first acquiring these foundations. Young people today, especially in the rush of modern life, find it unbearable to repeat the same exercise again and again, but this essential practice—the almost monotonous repetition of basic techniques—is the only sure foundation for effective Karate. Many beginners who come to learn Karate, dreaming of marvellous skill and prowess, give up only too soon, getting tired of repeating the simple but essential exercises.

It is no exaggeration to say that it is impossible to repeat these simple techniques too often. There is infinite meaning to be gained from their repetition. On the mental side, we can build up our character through the basic techniques of Karate, for through them we learn patience and concentration; on the physical side, we acquire bodily powers and control of our bodies, learning how to relax our shoulders in action, how to concentrate our energy on a single point or on a movement, how to twist our waist or our fist, and how to preserve perfect balance at all times.

It does not take long to acquire the actual foundation in principle, for this consists of only a few basic techniques; however, it involves such profundity of skill in practice that one may say that not even a lifetime would be enough to acquire perfection, or even near-perfection.

I have many recollections of hard but enjoyable training in which I repeated only the basic exercises for three hours without a break. Beginners should bear in mind that it is important to repeat each technique steadily and frequently—although this becomes a strain—since acquiring a proper foundation is essential for the development of more advanced techniques.

2. Points to Note

(a) *Avoiding a Strained Punch or Kick*

If you are too conscious of your opponent in punching or kicking, you will tend, in punching, to move only your hand and arm, unconsciously putting your weight and power into your shoulder, and pushing your bottom out to counterbalance. This is the worst possible posture. In it, not only is your speed impaired, but your intended movement is obvious to your opponent before it happens. In boxing this is known as telegraphing a punch. You cannot hope to be effective unless you overcome this tendency.

The most important point in this basic movement is to avoid making a strained punch or kick—that is, one which will not knock down the opponent at one blow. The essence of a successful punch or kick is that it is aimed at a point some twelve inches *inside* the opponent's body. In this way he will receive the full force of your blow. Think of thrusting a needle firmly into a piece of paper. The hole made by your needle forms just one spot, not a wide, ragged hole.

This is the kind of concentration you should aim for in your blows. If you strike at the surface of your opponent's body, your effort will be exhausted by the time your punch or kick reaches him. Have enough force left to thrust some twelve inches inside your target if it were a fixed object. Concentrate all of your energy on the blow, as if your entire body were one piece.

I think I have made my point clear. Now I want you to study the basic blows as shown in the illustrations, with explanations of the essential points.

(b) *Balance*

Keeping perfect balance at all times, especially after making an attack or block, is very important for your next movement of attack or block. If your balance is destroyed after a punch or kick, it is because wasteful energy has been exerted and the blow was strained. It is important to keep the weight concentrated in the lower part of the body, putting strength and power into the abdomen. If you put power into your shoulder, which means weight on the upper part of the body, your balance is vulnerable and easily destroyed.

(c) *Concentration*

Always keep your eyes concentrated on your opponent, and in practice always imagine an opponent in front of you. You must never look down, especially when making a rising block or a downward block, even if it is done while turning.

(d) *Twisting the Fist*

Punching in Karate is unique in that it is done with a twist. You must learn this punch in basic practice.

The punching hand must be placed above the hip-bone with the back of the hand facing downward. Thrust it straight forward, so that your elbow touches your side, then twist a little before impact on the target. At this point, especially, you must be certain not to lift your elbow, because if your elbow comes up, it means that you will put some of the power of the blow into your shoulder and the direction of your punch will not be straight, so that you will waste your energy and produce a punch which is not sharply focused.

(e) *Keeping the Wrist Straight: Clenching the Fist*

It is important to keep your wrist absolutely straight in punching. As beginners cannot clench their fists tightly, they tend to punch with their wrist bent. If they actually punch with a bent wrist, their punch is not only weak but their wrist will be damaged. As the photograph shows, you must clench your fingers tightly so that the line of the back of the hand makes a right or an acute angle with the striking point. It is necessary to practise clenching your fist tightly every day. For this practice it is a good idea to practise punching a rolled straw dummy.

(f) *Points to Watch in Kicking*

When kicking you must not straighten the knee of your supporting leg or lift your heel. This is for the sake of your balance: if your kick is blocked, you will be knocked over easily if your supporting leg is straightened or your heel lifted. You must be careful also not to lean over backward with the upper part of your body when kicking.

It is important to kick with the intention, as in punching, of using your entire body, not only your leg, to do so.

It is better for beginners to kick with the upper part of their body leaning slightly forward. It is not good to make a noise, bang, when you lower your kicking foot to the ground. It only means that you are wasting power and energy in your foot by doing this, and it makes it difficult for you to prepare your next move.

Kick with a snapping motion, and withdraw all power from the kicking foot after kicking immediately after the blow. Draw your foot back without unnecessary waste of energy: do not stamp your foot down. This will enable you to kick several times if you want to without shifting your balance or altering your posture. For this reason you should prepare your kicking posture with great care.

BASIC TECHNIQUES

There are eight forms of basic technique.

(a) *Junzuki* (*Forward Punch*)
This is a forward punching exercise.

(b) *Kette-Junzuki* (*Snap Kick and Forward Punch*)
This is a kicking and punching exercise.

(c) *Gyakuzuki* (*Reverse Punch*)
Reverse punching in the sense that the opposite arm is used to deliver the punch compared with the Junzuki punching stance.

(d) *Kette-Gyakuzuki* (*Snap Kick and Reverse Punch*)
The kicking action is the same as that in (b) but the punch is delivered with the opposite arm.

(e) *Junzuki-no-Tsukkomi* (*Forward Leaning Punch*)
This punch is delivered at the same time as the pace forward (same arm and leg).

(f) *Kette-Junzuki-no-Tsukkomi* (*Kick and Forward Leaning Punch*)
The leg moving forward is used to snap kick and then the forward leaning punch stance is adopted.

(g) *Gyakuzuki-no-Tsukkomi* (*Forward Leaning Reverse Punch*)
The step forward is 'wide' ending with a reverse punch with the body leaning forward.

(h) *Kette-Gyakuzuki-no-Tsukkomi* (*Kick and Forward Leaning Reverse Punch*)
Again the forward moving leg is used to snap kick and then the forward leaning reverse punch stance is adopted.

Comparing (a), (c), (e), and (g) we have the four basic punching techniques and (b), (d), (f), and (h) the four basic techniques with snap kick. As these exercises are all forward moving then it will be necessary to turn about to continue the exercises. There are two turning techniques, both practised on the assumption that an attack is being made from the rear, and they are therefore blocking techniques.

The first is Jodan Uke (Head Block)

next is Gedan Barai (Lower Block)

I am going to explain all the above exercises in some detail as it is essential to master the basic forms to help you to do some of the more difficult exercises correctly.

Junzuki (*See Figs. 51a, 51b.*)

This is the most basic of the stances and it is used very frequently. Study the pictures closely and try to adopt the same stance every time you step forward. Carry the weight forward first and then when the next step forward is finished—Punch.

The Posture of Junzuki

Note particularly (in Figs. 51a and 51b) the position of the arms, the straight wrists, the fist formation, the right fist held at the ready and the

Fig. 51a

Fig. 51b

Fig. 52a

Fig. 52b

Fig. 52c

Fig. 52d

Fig. 53a

Fig. 53b

position of the legs. Study the photographs carefully, and remember that balance is extremely important in Karate.

In the final position, as the punch is delivered the shoulder of the punching arm should be slightly forward compared to the other shoulder.

It is very important that the shoulders are completely relaxed during punching actions, strong punching being derived from the stomach and wrist. An incorrect stance is shown in Fig. 52a as well as tensed shoulders.

Fig. 52b shows another common mistake, with the feet in a straight line.

The weight should be evenly distributed over both legs, with the back straight. Figs. 52c and 52d show common faults. The rear leg should be straight but not tensed. The forward foot points straight ahead and the rear foot at an outward angle of approximately 45°. The head should be held erect with the eyes focused ahead on an imaginary opponent.

Zenshinshite Junzuki
(Moving forward in Junzuki or forward punch)

From the position of Fig. 51, the body is moved forward, with the left arm extended in the punching position, taking a pace forward with the right foot, left knee slightly bent as the weight is carried forward, to the position of the legs in Fig. 53a.

Up to this point the right arm is held at the ready position. Once the stance of Fig. 53a is adopted, the punch with the right fist is delivered, ending in the position shown. At the same time the left arm is withdrawn to the ready position at the hips (see Fig. 53b).

POINTS TO WATCH

1. The whole of the body is moved at the same time in the step forward, not just the legs, or arms with legs trailing. Figs. 52c and 52d show incorrect posture. Both are common and recurring faults and show practically everything done incorrectly.

2. The wrist movement when punching.

To punch correctly it is essential that the twisting motion is done at the correct time and this applies to both the forward punch and retracting the arm which had punched previously to the ready position, i.e. on the hips with thumb uppermost.

Fig. 54 shows the change in progress. Here a punch is to be delivered with the right fist, and note that the thumb is still uppermost while it is travelling forward. It will remain in this position until only a few inches from the target and then the wrist is turned quickly anti-clockwise just before striking to enable the thumb to be downwards on contact. The left fist has remained as it was from the previous contact and will be turned again anti-clockwise near its rest position at the left hip. Both these twisting motions are simultaneous. The procedure is repeated after the next step forward but of course the twisting motion is then clockwise. It is strange that the strength applied to the withdrawing arm should be greater than that applied to the punching arm, but this is so, as you will realize when you practise punching. A strong withdrawal of the retracting arm adds momentum to the forward punch.

Finally, I must remind you that the forward movement of the punch is of course timed to coincide with the withdrawal of the other arm, and is achieved as quickly as possible. Many students, however, are apt to withdraw too quickly, or incorrectly, thus reducing the power of their punch.

Kette-Junzuki

From the position shown in Fig. 51 kick forward with the rear foot, withdrawing it slightly after the kick is completed, move the body forward and deliver the forward punch, Junzuki. Fig. 55a shows the first move from Fig. 51 position.

Fig. 54

Fig. 55a

Fig. 55b

Fig. 56a

Fig. 56b

Fig. 57

Fig. 58

Fig. 59

Fig. 60

Fig. 61

Fig. 62

Fig. 63a

Fig. 63b

Diag. 4

Diag. 5

Fig. 63c

The front view is Fig. 55b.

Fig. 56a shows the completed kick. (Note the toes are well back.) The front view is shown in Fig. 56b.

You must pay strict attention to the following points:

1. When kicking, the foot must be drawn up to the kicking position first. (*See Figs. 55a and b.*) Fig. 57 shows a common mistake with beginners when they kick as if kicking a football.

2. Relax the shoulders. The whole body should in fact be relaxed. If the body is tense, particularly the shoulders, then no power will be developed in the punch or kick. Fig. 58 shows the incorrect way.

3. The instep should be stretched straight. (*See Fig. 56a.* Fig. 59 shows a wrong kick.)

4. The toes of the kicking foot must be bent back, kicking only with the ball of the foot. Fig. 60 shows the wrong kick, which would result in broken toes.

5. Always aim the ball of the foot at the imaginary opponent's stomach. Fig. 61 shows a kick wildly out of alignment, but this is a common occurrence with beginners.

6. Kick with the supporting knee slightly bent (refer to Fig. 56a), and *do not* stretch or lean backwards. *See Fig. 62.*

The above six points are essential for correct balance and kicking power, so study them closely.

Gyakuzuki (See Figs. 63a, 63b. Diagram 4.)

The Posture of Gyakuzuki

(1) From the posture of Junzuki you would be commanded to reverse your punch (Sonobade Ippon Toru) bringing you to the Gyakuzuki posture. You would therefore begin from the Junzuki stance and first start the punching change-over, i.e. withdraw left fist to the ready position on the left hip and at the same time punch with the right fist. Simultaneously you must turn your forward foot slightly inwards and pull it slightly backwards and outwards, with the rear toes slightly inwards.

The foot moves occur at the same instant as the extremity of the punch is reached and, in consequence, the hips twist into the direction of the punch, giving added momentum. Again it is important that the previously outstretched arm (in Junzuki) is retracted at the same speed as the forward punch.

(2) The weight must be evenly proportioned over the legs, and the body (particularly the shoulders) relaxed.

(3) The knees should be tensed inwards slightly. *See Fig. 63a.*

Moving Forward from the Gyakuzuki Stance (See Diagram 5.)

Particular attention should be paid to the move forward as in Junzuki but in addition watch the following points.

(1) When stepping forward twist the leading foot outwards (*see Figs. 63c, 63d*) and twist the body outwards as well. (*Diagram 4.*) Fig. 63c is the start of the move forward, from the stance of Fig. 63a which shows the path the foot is to travel ending in Fig. 63e. At this point in the step forward you will note that the left fist is still in the ready position, and the previous punching arm is still extended.

(2) (*Diagram 5.*) The moment that the toes of the forward foot touch (*Fig. 63e*) the punch starts, the left hip twists forward causing the right hip to twist to the rear, this in turn brings the right heel inwards and the foot slightly back and outwards timed to occur at the extremity of the punch. *Figs. 63f, 63g.*

The power in the punch is obtained by the rapid hip movement mentioned above, and without this and the foot movement the punching technique is not correct. Fig. 64 shows a bad stance.

Fig. 63d

Fig. 63e

Fig. 63f

Fig. 63g

Fig. 64

Fig. 65a

Fig. 65b

Fig. 66

Fig. 67

Fig. 68

Fig. 69a

Fig. 69b

44

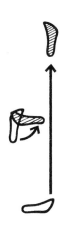

Diag. 6

Fig. 69c

Fig. 70a

Fig. 70b

Kette-Gyakuzuki (See Figs. 65a, 65b.)

The kick is started from the stance of Fig. 63c using the rear foot and with the body twisted slightly outwards. Note the bent supporting leg. Beginners tend to kick outwards, so study Fig. 65a closely.

After the delivery of the kick the foot is dropped to the position of Fig. 63e and the punch completed as for Gyakuzuki.

Junzuki-no-Tsukkomi (Fig. 66.)

Posture

(1) The completed punch is shown in Fig. 66, and reference to Diagram 6 shows the position of the feet. The body weight is shifted forward and supported on the front leg which is bent. (*See Diagram 6.*)

(2) The rear leg should be straight and the lower part of the front leg vertical. Fig. 67 shows a usual beginner's type of stance with the front leg incorrect.

(3) The punching arm should be pointing straight at the face region of the opponent, and the fist about the same height as the eyes.

(4) The hips should be moved into the line of the punch but the hip movement should not be overdone.

(5) The upper part of the body should be leaning forward not to the point of bad balance, but in a natural stance. An incorrect but nevertheless common stance is shown in Fig. 68.

(6) The distance between the feet should be 8 in. or so greater than the basic Junzuki stance.

The correct way to step forward to deliver Junzuki-no-Tsukkomi. See Figs. 69a, 69b, 69c. The step forward is taken, ensuring that the feet end in the correct position with body slightly forward. The punch is then delivered. Again the hips are used to add power to the punch and are slightly twisted into the punch for this purpose.

The punching arm is held in position until the next step forward is started. The arm is then withdrawn at the same time as the body moves forward and the opposite punch is delivered.

Kette-Junzuki-no-Tsukkomi (See Figs. 70a, 70b, 70c, 70d.)

To kick with the rear foot from the basic *Junzuki-no-Tsukkomi* stance is difficult unless the body is twisted to be forward facing (Fig. 70a) and the kick delivered from this position (Fig. 70c).

The kick is a snap kick and the foot is dropped to the stance for the punching position of Fig. 69a.

Gyakuzuki-no-Tsukkomi (See Figs. 71a, 71b. Diagram 7.)

Posture

(1) The position of the feet.

The heel of the forward foot should be in line with the toes of the rear foot. The distance between the feet is approximately equal to twice the width of the shoulders.

(2) The rear leg should be straight with the toes of the foot pointing slightly inwards.

(3) The upper part of the body should be leaning slightly forward with the punch directed at the lower part of the opponent's stomach.

(4) The knees are tensed inwards in a similar posture to Gyakuzuki.

Fig. 70c

Fig. 70d

Fig. 71a

Fig. 71b

Fig. 72a

Fig. 72b

Fig. 72c

Fig. 72d

Fig. 72e

Fig. 72f

Fig. 73

Fig. 74a

Diag. 7

Diag. 8

Fig. 74b

Fig. 74c

Stepping Forward to Deliver (Gyakuzuki-no-Tsukkomi) (See Figs. 71, 72a–f.)

(1) Starting from the correct stance of Fig. 71 the front foot is turned outwards as the body is twisted slightly in the same direction. The rear foot points in the same direction as the front foot. *See Figs. 72a and 72b*. The rear foot then completes the forward movement, following the path of a deep 'V' at right angles to the forward movement of the technique with the apex near to the heel of the supporting foot. *See Figs. 72c and 72d*.

(2) When the heel of the forward foot touches the floor the hips are again twisted into the punch, so aiding the blow. *See Figs. 72e and 72f*. The punch should always be directed to the front and not waver during the move forward. Most beginners generally punch sideways because of incorrect posture.

Kette-Gyakuzuki-no-Tsukkomi (See Fig. 73, Figs. 72a and 72b.)

The hips should be twisted outwards to snap kick to the front with the rear foot.

Beginners are again apt to kick sideways but it is necessary to use the hips to produce a correct forward-facing snap kick.

The body should be leaning forward slightly to deliver the kick and should never be upright. After kicking the foot should be withdrawn slightly and a step sideways taken. *See Fig. 73*.

Then the punch is delivered.

Uke or Blocking Techniques

The following blocking techniques assume an attack is being made from the rear.

Jodan Uke (Head Block) (See Figs. 74a–f, Figs. 75a–c. Diagram 8.)

This move is intended to block an attack to the head from behind.

The basic stance from which the block is made is that of the Junzuki punching techniques, and results in a complete turn about to confront a would-be attacker with a defensive move. The turn must be accomplished quickly to be effective. Diagram 8 shows the position of the feet in the Junzuki stance prior to turning.

For the turn, the rear foot is moved across (Fig. 74a), still holding the punching arm extended.

Fig. 74b shows the side view of the move. From the position of Fig. 74a the body is pivoted around on the toes to that shown in Fig. 74c and Diagram 5. At this point the left arm is partially withdrawn and the fist previously held at the ready position on the hip is moving forward to that shown in Fig. 74d (rear view) and Figs. 74e and 74f. Note that the ready hand is in *front* of the previous punching hand.

Figs. 75a, b, and c show the completion of the block. Diagram 6. Study the photographs carefully, note the position of the legs. This is the Junzuki stance but the right arm in the pictures is protecting the head and the left arm is in the ready position.

POINTS TO WATCH

(1) That the blocking forearm is raised to its final position with an outward 'twist' of the wrist and is protecting the forehead. The power comes from the twisting action.

(2) The wrist should be straight and shoulders relaxed.

(3) The stance is the same as Junzuki.

Gedan Barai (Rear Sweeping Block) (See Figs. 76, 77, 78, 79.)

Here is an explanation of Gedan Barai with the right hand, starting from the Gyakuzuki position.

The right foot, which is at the rear, is moved to the left. *See Diagram 9 from (1) to (2)*. This movement is done with the foot only. The right

continued on page 50

Fig. 74d

Fig. 74e

Fig. 74f

Fig. 75a

Fig. 75b

Fig. 75c

Fig. 76a

Fig. 76b

Fig. 76c

Fig. 77a

Fig. 77b

Fig. 78a

Fig. 78b

Fig. 79a

Fig. 79b

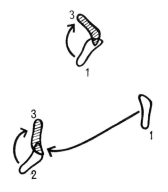

Diag. 9

Diag. 10

| Fig. 80 | Wrong View | Fig. 81 | Wrong View | Fig. 82 | Wrong View |

hand is lightly placed in front of the left chest with the thumb uppermost. The left knee must remain bent and the hips kept low to maintain balance. *See Figs. 76a, b, and c.* The face is turned to the opponent behind, the hips are twisted and the attacking front kick is blocked with the right hand, making full use of the twisting of the hips. *See Figs. 77a, b, 78a, b, 79a, b. Diagram 10.*

POINTS TO WATCH

(1) If the twisting of the hips is not sufficient, the block will not be effective. *See Fig. 80.* The stance is the same as Junzuki.

(2) The blocking hand must not stop short or the attack may strike the leg. *See Fig. 81.*

(3) Too much strength must not be used in blocking because it will break the balance. *See Fig. 82.*

All the blocks should be sufficient to protect the defender with the minimum effort, for strength must be preserved for the counter-attack.

6 KATA FORM

1. The Meaning of Kata Form

'Kata' in Karate refers to the art of combining in a sequence of moves all the attacking and blocking techniques of Karate in a rational and highly skilled and refined manner. The nearest English word equivalent to kata is 'form'. It is clear from a study of the 'form' of Karate how Karate evolved and developed as an art of self-defence. There are many kinds of 'form', all of which start with defence. This shows that every move in Karate developed out of the need for self-defence against attack.

2. Characteristics of Form

The advantage of Karate 'form' exercises is that we can practise them by ourselves, anytime, anywhere. They are an excellent way of keeping fit, for every muscle is exerted correctly and to its maximum potential. For older people, as well as women and children, they are a way of preserving and developing physical strength and alertness, while young people can exercise their strength, and at the same time they learn self-defence.

3. Points to Note

It is said that in the old days each form was practised by itself thoroughly for three years; there is a Japanese saying, 'one form in three years'. This emphasizes the fact that it is more important to master one form correctly than to learn many forms insufficiently.

It is useless to exercise mechanically without understanding the meaning of what you are doing. You should first understand the meaning of form and then practise your form exercises in a 'living' way, always imagining an opponent. For example, the movements of each form must flow one into the other and if you do not know the meaning of each form as a whole, you will not know what you are doing or why. Of course, this sequence of techniques must be followed carefully and properly.

4. Kushanku (Chinese: Kung, Hsiang-chün)

It is said that this form is named after a Chinese, Kung, Hsiang-chün, who introduced it to Okinawa. This is a wonderful exercise: it is one of the longest forms of all and has been designed very rationally. It consists of a variety of attacking and blocking techniques against imagined enemies in every direction. If you practise only this form thoroughly, you will not need to learn many other forms. In this form, you can learn quick changes of technique, slowness and quickness, application and withdrawal of power, maintenance of balance, stretching and bending the body, correct breathing, body shifting, and combination of techniques of hands and feet, etc.

KUSHANKU KATA (FORM)

There are eight directions in this Kata as Diagram 11 shows, and no more, therefore this Kata must only move in these eight directions.

See Fig. 83. The first position.

See Fig. 84 and Diagram 12. The ready position. First move the left foot to the left and then the right foot to the right slowly, standing with the left hand crossed over the right—both hands open.

Note 1. The distance between the feet must be as wide as the shoulders.

Note 2. The crossed hands should be under slight tension and placed a little away from the body to be ready for the next movement.

See Fig. 85. From the ready position raise the arms above the head without bending the arms.

Note 1. Relax the shoulders.

Note 2. Raise the arms *slowly*.

See Fig. 86. The thumbs are now bent and the hands strong.

See Fig. 87. The arms are now lowered with the palms facing outwards describing a circle. As Fig. 87 shows, the thumbs are bent with the tips of the fingers touching. (This has two meanings. The first is to show the Deity that you have no weapon in your hand. The second is that the circular movement means peace, showing that Karate students realize the value of peace.)

See Figs. 88a and b, and Diagram 13. Against an attack to the left side of the face move the left foot slightly to the left, raise the heel, and lower the waist into the *Nekoashi* (Cat stance). Lift the left hand in an arc and block with the back of the hand. At the same time bring the left hand to the middle as shown.

Note 1. The body must face the front.

Note 2. The face only must turn to the left.

Nekoashi Stance. The body weight must be distributed about 60% or 70% on the back foot and the legs must be bent as much as possible. The heel of the front foot must be raised and the foot facing straight ahead. The back must be kept straight.

See Fig. 89 and Diagram 14. From (C) pull the left foot back to (a) and from (B) move the right foot to (d).

This technique is the opposite to the preceding one (Fig. 88). From Fig. 88 the left and right arms are straightened, the feet are changed and the arms are brought across the body. The right arm is moved quickly up to block the attacking punch with the back hand and the left hand is pulled into position across the body.

See Fig. 90 and Diagram 15. Move right from (a) to (b) and straighten both legs. This stance is the same as the ready position. The right hand is clenched and placed on the hip while the left hand, also clenched, is moved across the body, being placed in position without touching the body or the right fist.

See Fig. 91. The left fist is moved forward quickly to block a punch to the stomach with the forearm.

See Fig. 92. The left hand is pulled back and the right punches for the attacker's stomach at the same time.

See Fig. 93a and Diagram 16. The left foot moves to the left and the right arm moves down and to the left with a relaxed movement. The left knee is bent and the right knee is straightened.

Note. Keep the body facing the front.

See Fig. 93b. Twist the hips to the left.

See Fig. 93c. At the same time bring up the right arm and block with

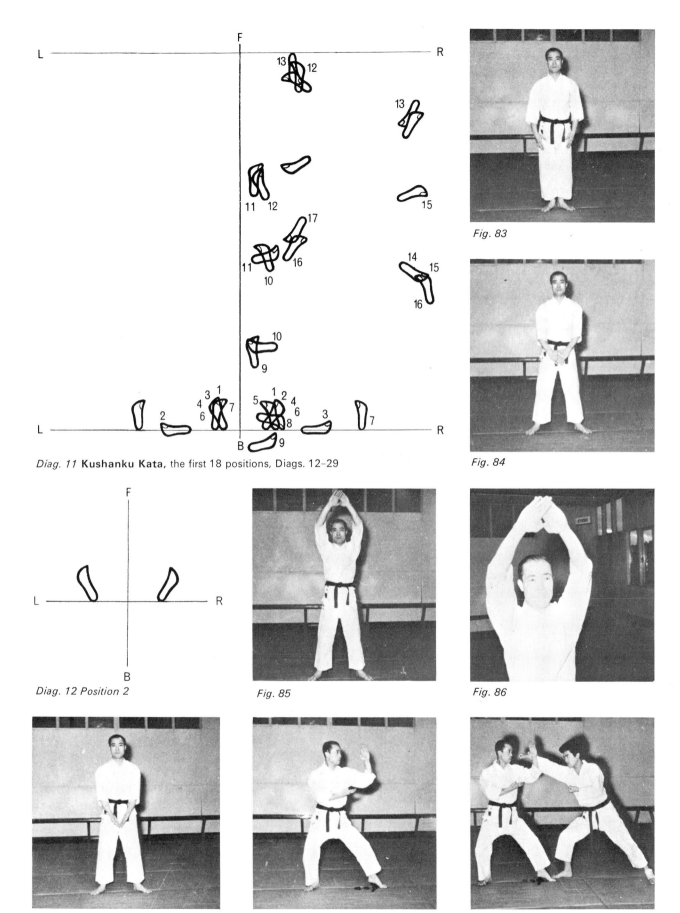

Diag. 11 **Kushanku Kata**, the first 18 positions, Diags. 12–29

Fig. 83

Fig. 84

Diag. 12 Position 2

Fig. 85

Fig. 86

Fig. 87

Fig. 88a

Fig. 88b

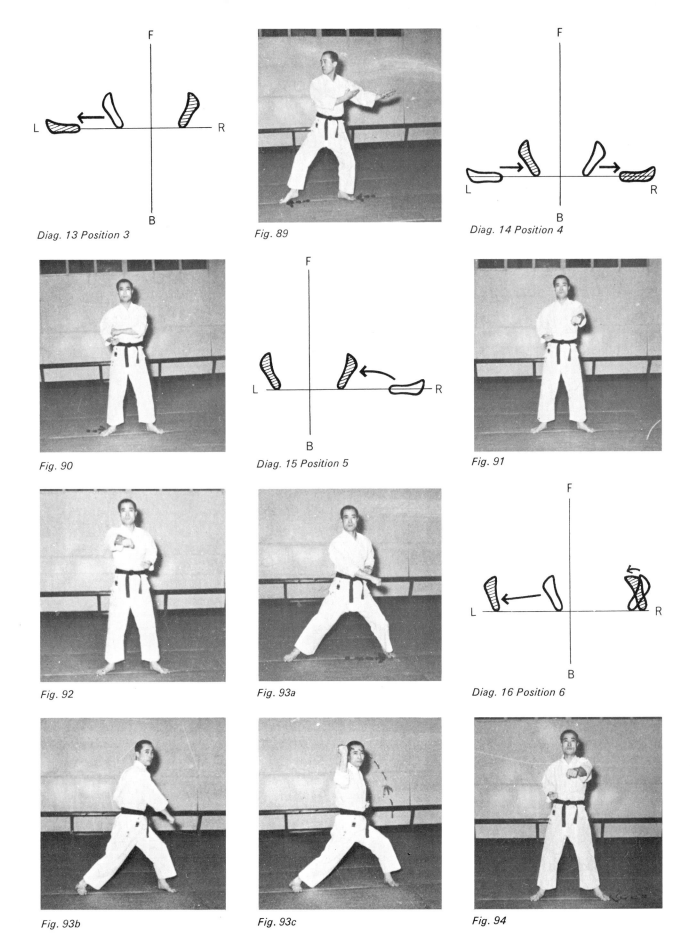

Diag. 13 Position 3

Fig. 89

Diag. 14 Position 4

Fig. 90

Diag. 15 Position 5

Fig. 91

Fig. 92

Fig. 93a

Diag. 16 Position 6

Fig. 93b

Fig. 93c

Fig. 94

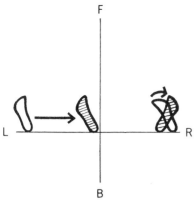

Diag. 17 Position 7

Fig. 95

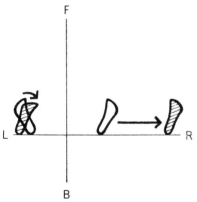

Diag. 18 Position 8

Fig. 96a

the forearm an attack to the face (*Diagram 15*). Note that when the hips are twisted to the left, the right foot is turned inwards.

See Fig. 94 and Diagram 17. The left leg is moved to the right in the ready position as Fig. 84. The legs are straightened and the right arm is brought down to a position on the hips. At the same time the left arm punches to the attacker's stomach.

Note 1. As the hips are twisted and the arm rises for the block the shoulders must be relaxed.

Note 2. Figs. 92, 93, and 94 are practised as one movement.

Note 3. The body must not lean forward or back but must be kept upright, and the right heel must be kept on the ground.

See Fig. 95 and Diagram 18. This is the opposite movement to Figs. 92, 93, 94, and 96.

See Figs. 96a and b, and Diagram 19a. Pull down left hand to the left hip. From the right hip the right arm is relaxed and placed slightly across the body with the back of the hand facing upwards. At the same time the feet are moved as in Diagram 18 and the hips are twisted to the right with the head turned facing the rear.

See Fig. 97. The right arm is quickly brought up into *Soto Uke* (Outside block) to the rear. See Diagram 19b which shows the part of the arm used in this block. At the same time front kick also to the rear.

See Figs. 98a and b, and Diagram 20. Move feet as in Diagram 20. At the same time open the hands, keeping the thumbs bent and strong, lift the left hand up to the right ear, twisting the hand inwards and the right arm straight out to the side, palm downwards. The body is in the same position as before.

See Figs. 99a and b. Twist the hips to the left and at the same time the left hand moves across the face, twisting the hand so that the palm faces outwards. The hand and forearm are kept straight upwards. At the same time the right arm moves across the body, twisting until the palm faces upwards. This technique is called knifehand block.

Note 1. The blocking hand must be held near the face.

Note 2. Figs. 96, 97, 98, and 99 are practised as one movement.

Note 3. The *Soto Uke* (Block) must be taken right across the face otherwise the attacking punch will still strike the face.

Note 4. Figs. 99a and 99b are in the 'cat' stance and the front foot must be straight and in line with the heel of the back foot.

Note 5. In the 'cat' stance the body must face 45° to the side and not frontwards.

Note 6. Keep the shoulders relaxed.

See Figs. 100a and b, and Diagram 21. Move the feet as in Diagram 21. At the same time bring up the right hand into the knifehand block and the left hand across the body in the opposite movement to Fig. 96.

See Fig. 101. This is a photograph showing the incorrect way of moving the arms—the right arm must be brought up to the left ear before being moved into the knifehand block.

See Fig. 99a and Diagram 22. The body moves forward one step with the same stance and knifehand block.

See Figs. 102a, b, and c, and Diagram 23. Move forward with the right foot into Junzuki stance, the right hand, open with the thumb strongly bent, strikes with spearhand.

Note. Do not pull the hand back before striking with spearhand.

See Figs. 103a and b, and Diagram 24a. The left leg is moved to the right and the right hand is moved to the forehead with the palm outwards

continued on page 59

Fig. 96b

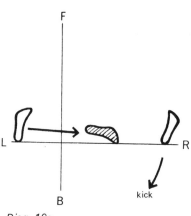

Diag. 19a

Fig. 97

Diag. 19b

Fig. 98a

Fig. 98b

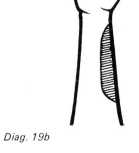

Diag. 20 Position 9

Fig. 99a

Fig. 99b

Fig. 100a

Fig. 100b

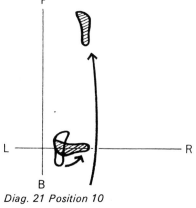

Diag. 21 Position 10

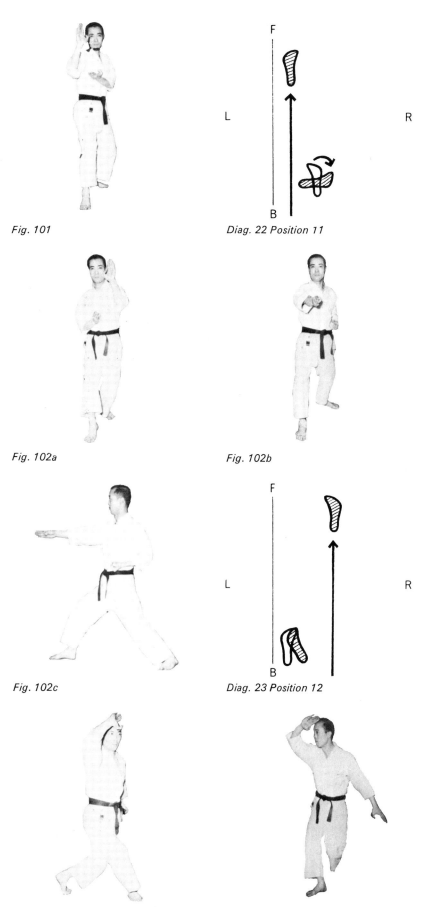

Fig. 101

Diag. 22 Position 11

Fig. 102a

Fig. 102b

Fig. 102c

Diag. 23 Position 12

Fig. 103a

Fig. 103b

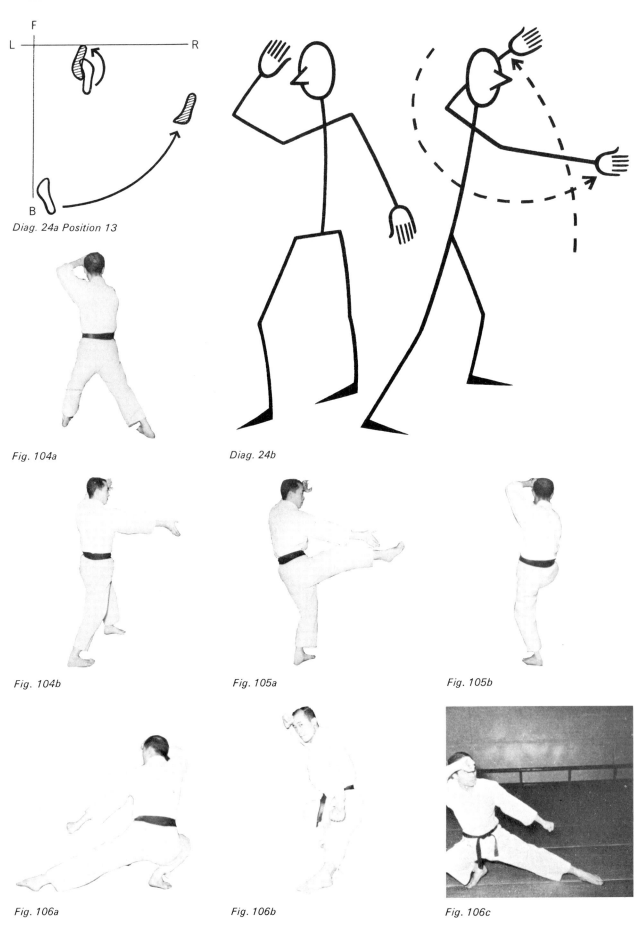

Diag. 24a Position 13

Fig. 104a

Diag. 24b

Fig. 104b

Fig. 105a

Fig. 105b

Fig. 106a

Fig. 106b

Fig. 106c

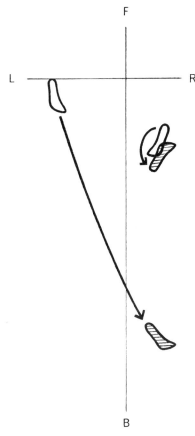

Diag. 25 Position 14

Fig. 107

Fig. 108

and the thumb strongly bent. The left hand is opened and straightened away from the body with the back of the hand upwards.

See Figs. 104a and b. Twist the hips strongly to the left and turn the body to the rear, at the same time the right hand moves from the forehead in an arc to the front, and blocks an attacker's punch with the palm of the hand. The left hand moves straight up to the forehead with the palm facing outwards. *See Diagram 24b.*

Note 1. See Diagram 24a. The toe of the right foot must be almost in line with the heel of the left foot.

Note 2. All the techniques up to now have been moving to the front. Now the body is turned and the techniques are moving in the opposite direction.

See Figs. 105a and b. Right front foot kick to the stomach.

See Figs. 106a, b, and c, and Diagram 25. After the kick, bring the right foot straight down and bend the knee lowering the body as in Fig. 106a, keeping the left leg straight with the foot flat on the floor. The heel of the right foot is raised. At the same time the left hand is clenched and the arm straightened into the lower block against an attacker's kick. The right hand is clenched and brought up to the forehead.

See Fig. 107. The right hand is moved in an arc to a position above the left knee, blocking an attacker's kick with the forearm. The left fist moves up to the right shoulder.

See Fig. 108 and Diagram 26. Straighten the right leg and bring up the left leg to a position about the width of the shoulders apart from the right. At the same time the left hand moves across the body to the side and blocks with the forearm. The right arm is pulled back to a position on the right hip. The face is turned to the left side of the body. The body faces right.

Note. When the body is raised for the right block, the hips must be twisted strongly to the right and the shoulders relaxed.

See Diagram 27. The left leg is moved back and to the right and the body is turned 90° to the left. Then use the same technique as Fig. 104b but with the body facing the front.

The next techniques are the same as Figs. 105 to 107 but in reverse. In this stance the body faces left.

See Diagrams 28 and 29. This shows the position of the feet at the end of the previous technique.

See Fig. 109 and Diagrams 30 and 31. Turn the body 90°. Bring the feet together as Diagram 30. The left hand moves across the body above the right hand which stays on the right hip.

Note. The left hand does not touch the body and is also kept clear of the right hand.

See Fig. 110. The left hand moves to the left side with the arm straight into a forearm block against an attacker's punch to the middle. At the same time the left leg kicks to the left side.

See Fig. 111. This is incorrect. The left arm has blocked too high and the attacker's punch has struck the body.

See Fig. 112 and Diagram 32. After the kick the left leg is lowered to the front, the body is twisted to the left and a punch is delivered with the right elbow.

Note. This stance is the same as for the Gyakuzuki.

See Fig. 113 and Diagram 33. The right foot is drawn up to the left.

See Diagram 33. Keep the knees straight.

See Figs. 114a and b, and Diagram 34. This is the opposite technique to Figs. 109 to 112.

See Fig. 115 and Diagram 35. Turn the body 180° to the left and, with the left knifehand, block an attack from the rear.

continued on page 63

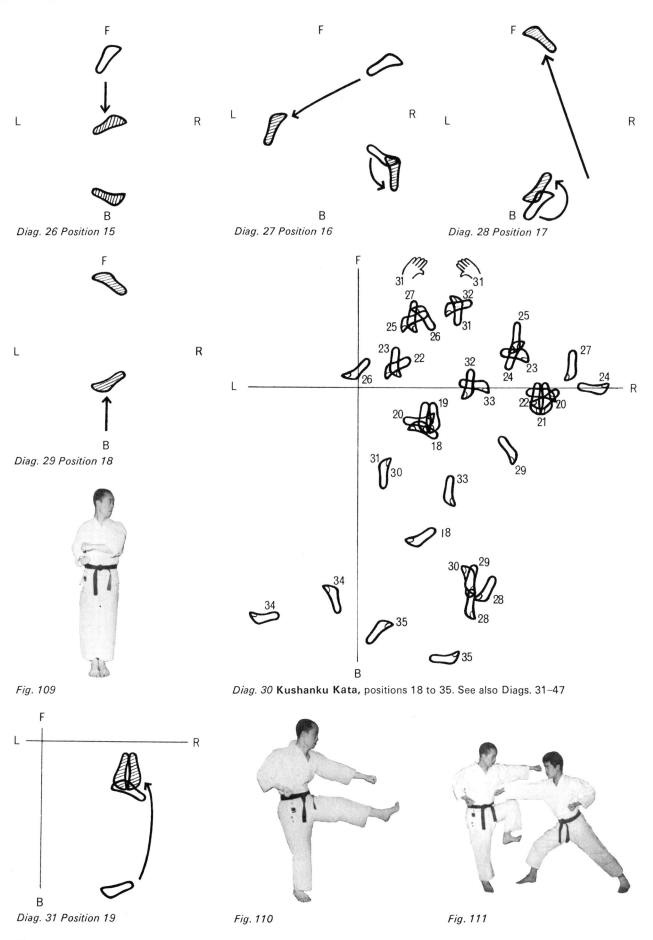

Diag. 26 Position 15

Diag. 27 Position 16

Diag. 28 Position 17

Diag. 29 Position 18

Fig. 109

Diag. 30 **Kushanku Kata,** positions 18 to 35. See also Diags. 31–47

Diag. 31 Position 19

Fig. 110

Fig. 111

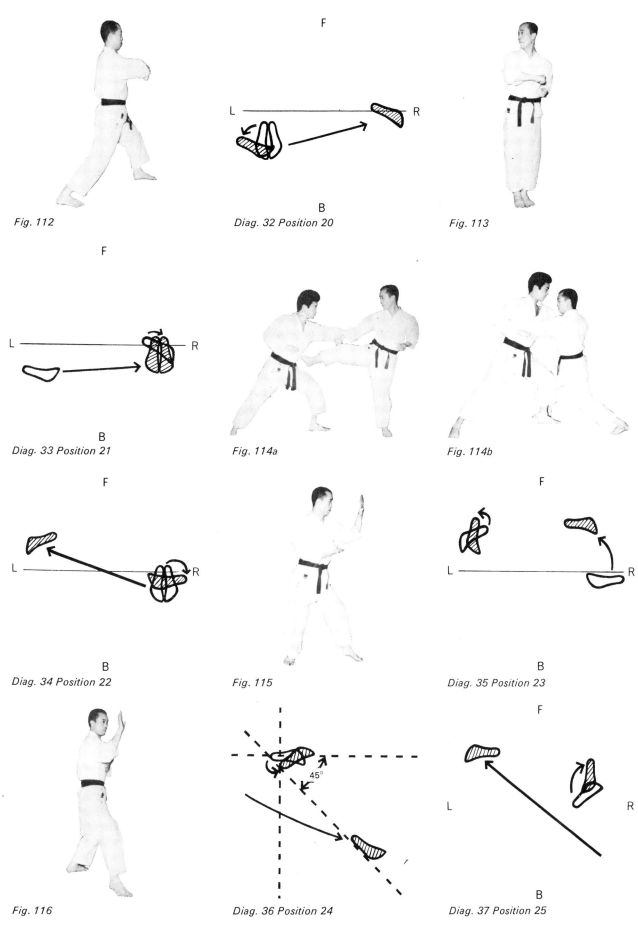

Fig. 112

F

Diag. 32 Position 20

B

Fig. 113

F

L — R

B

Diag. 33 Position 21

Fig. 114a

Fig. 114b

F

Diag. 34 Position 22

B

Fig. 115

F

Diag. 35 Position 23

B

Fig. 116

Diag. 36 Position 24

45°

Diag. 37 Position 25

F

L   R

B

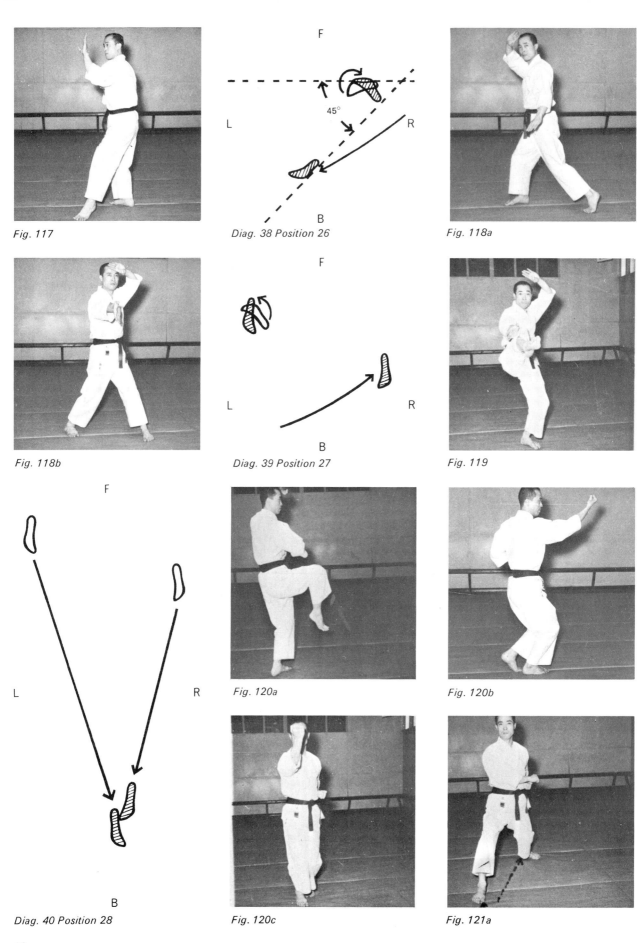

Fig. 117

Diag. 38 Position 26

Fig. 118a

Fig. 118b

Diag. 39 Position 27

Fig. 119

Diag. 40 Position 28

Fig. 120a

Fig. 120b

Fig. 120c

Fig. 121a

Fig. 121b

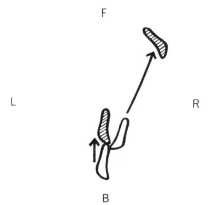

Diag. 41 Position 29

Fig. 122a

Fig. 122b

See Fig. 116 and Diagram 36. Move to the right 45° and block with the right knifehand.

See Diagram 37. Move to the right with the right foot and turn the body right. The right hand moves up to the left ear, then once more blocks with right knifehand. At the same time the left hand moves straight out to the side, then it is brought across the body, twisting the hand until the palm is facing upwards.

See Fig. 117 and Diagram 38. The left foot moves forward 45° to the left, and then left knifehand block.

See Figs. 118a and b, and Diagram 39. The left leg moves as in drawing and the body is turned to the left. This technique is the same as from Figs. 103 to 104b.

See Fig. 119. Right front kick as in Fig. 105, but facing the opposite direction.

See Figs. 120a, b, and c, and Diagram 40. This kick is a snap kick after which the right foot is moved forward before touching the floor, and the left foot is brought up to it with the heel raised. At the same time the right hand moves forward and strikes the attacker's face with the back fist. The left hand is pulled on to the left hip.

Note 1. The back fist is moved up from the waist in a forward circle.

Note 2. When the left foot is brought up to the right, the knees are together and the hips are kept low.

See Figs. 121a and b, and Diagram 41. Move the left foot a long step back then move the right foot back slightly. At the same time bring the right arm down and across the body, then block with right outside block.

Note 1. This stance is Junzuki.

Note 2. Do not move the left hand.

See Figs. 122a, b, and c. Left and right double straight punch to the stomach.

See Figs. 123a, b, and c, and Diagram 42. Move the left foot back and to the right and turn 180° to the left facing the opposite direction. The right foot twists on the ball of the foot. At the same time both arms are straightened to the sides with the left hand open and the right hand still clenched.

See Figs. 124a and b. The right knee is raised and the hands are quickly brought forward in front of the body, with the back of the left hand facing left and the back of the right fist downwards. The palm of the left hand and the bottom of the right fist strike the knee then lift slightly and come together in front of the chest. The back must be kept straight during this movement.

See Figs. 125a and b, and Diagram 43. The right leg moves forward a pace and the hands are placed on the floor, level with the shoulders and with the fingertips and thumbs on the floor but the palms raised. The arms are bent and the body lowered against an attack from the rear. The left leg is kept straight and both heels are raised.

See Fig. 126 and Diagram 44. Bring up the left foot slightly and at the same time lift the body and turn 180° to the left. Block with left knifehand, the stance being *Nekoashi* (Cat stance). For knifehand block see Fig. 99. Figs. 123 to 126 are practised as one movement as the student becomes more proficient.

See Fig. 127 and Diagram 45. Step forward with the right foot and block once more with knifehand.

See Figs. 128a and b, and Diagram 46. Turn to the left 270° and take a long step forward with the left foot and bring the right foot up into *Nekoashi* stance. On the turn the arms move as in Fig. 128, then as the

continued on page 67

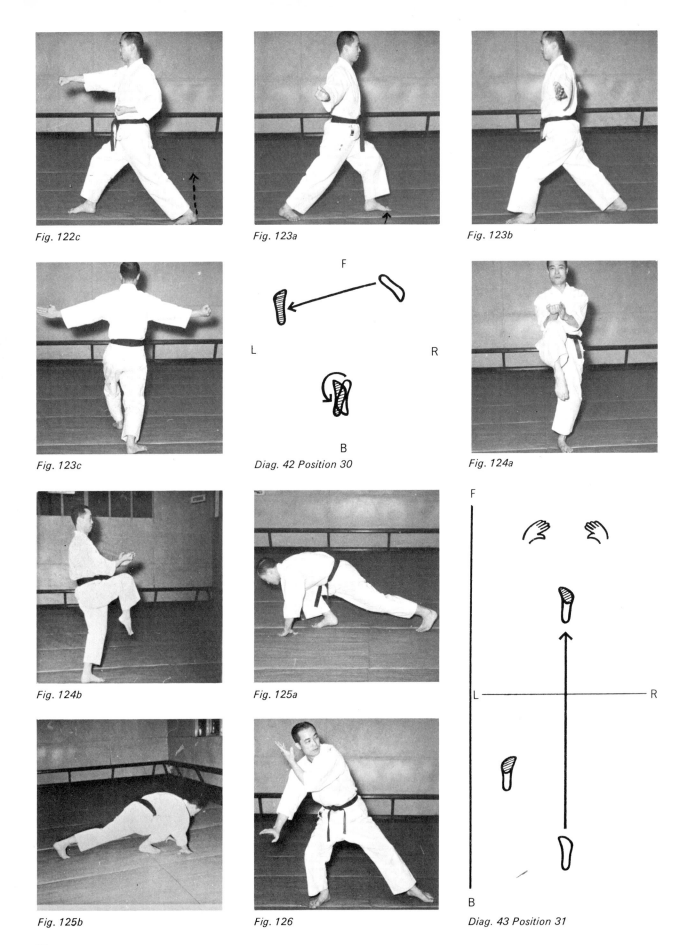

Fig. 122c

Fig. 123a

Fig. 123b

Fig. 123c

Diag. 42 Position 30

Fig. 124a

Fig. 124b

Fig. 125a

Fig. 125b

Fig. 126

Diag. 43 Position 31

Diag. 44 Position 32

Fig. 127

Diag. 45 Position 33

Fig. 128a

Fig. 128b

Diag. 46 Position 34

Fig. 129

Fig. 130a

Fig. 130b

Diag. 47 Position 35

Fig. 131

Fig. 132

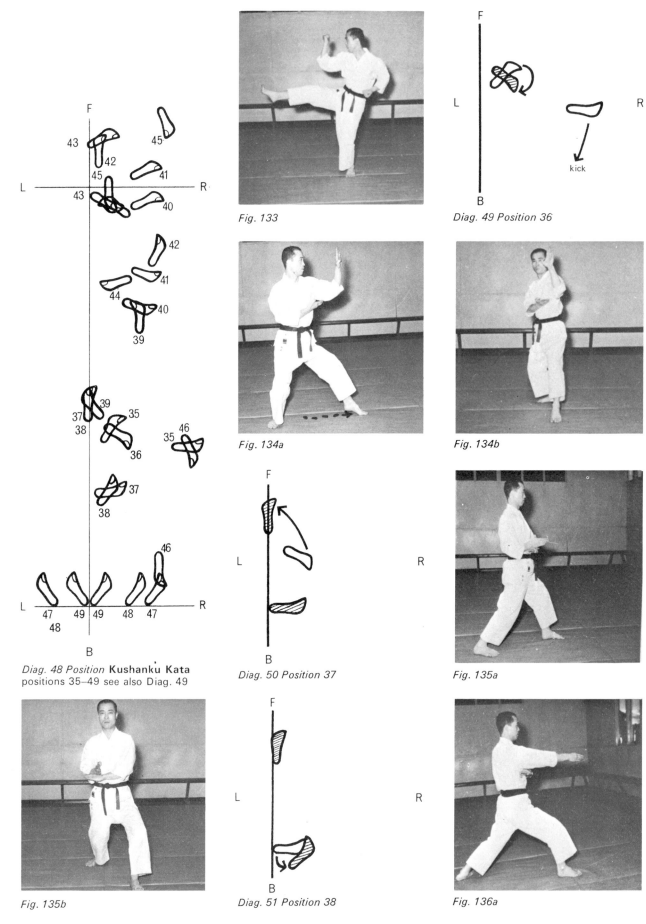

Fig. 133

Diag. 49 Position 36

Fig. 134a

Fig. 134b

Diag. 48 Position **Kushanku Kata**
positions 35–49 see also Diag. 49

Diag. 50 Position 37

Fig. 135a

Fig. 135b

Diag. 51 Position 38

Fig. 136a

Fig. 136b

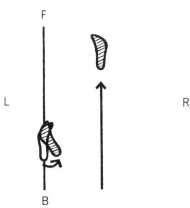
Diag. 52 Position 39

Fig. 137a

Fig. 137b

Fig. 138a

Fig. 138b

feet move into *Nekoashi* stance, the hands move up into the outside block.

Note. To do the outside block correctly, full use must be made of the hip twist.

See Fig. 129. The feet are kept still while the right hand moves forward into the reverse punch and the left hand is pulled back to the left hip.

See Figs. 130a and b, and Diagram 47. The left heel is lowered and the right hand comes across the body. The body moves in a turn of 180° to the right. The right foot takes a long step and the left foot comes up into *Nekoashi* stance. The right arm moves up into outside block. This movement is the opposite to the previous one. The left hand does not move during this technique.

See Fig. 131. Punch with the left and right hand alternately.

See Fig. 132. Turn 90° to the right then relax the right hand and lower it.

See Fig. 133 and Diagram 49. Raise the right arm quickly in outside block against an attack to the face. At the same time deliver a front kick to the solar plexus.

See Figs. 134a and b, and Diagram 50. Lower the right foot and turn to the left 180° into left knifehand block. The feet are in *Nekoashi* stance. (This technique is the same as Figs. 96 to 99.)

See Figs. 135a and b, and Diagram 51. Twist the hips to the front and pull down the left knifehand to a position across the body level with hips, with the back of the hand upwards. The right hand moves into spearhand, touching the body, and on top of the left hand. The stance is *Junzuki.*

See Figs. 136a and b, and Diagram 52. Step forward with the right foot into *Junzuki* stance and strike with spearhand attack to the stomach. The left hand does not move.

See Figs. 137a and b. Twist the right hand clockwise and move the upper body forward and sideways. (The hand must not be pulled back.)

See Figs. 138a and b, and Diagram 53. The left leg moves back and to the left and the body turns 180° to the left. The stance is *Shikodachi* and the attacker is punched in the solar plexus with the left bottom fist. The right hand is pulled back to the right hip.

See Figs. 139a, b, c, and d. This is the same technique photographed from the front.

See Figs. 140a and b, and Diagram 54. Bring the left fist up to the right ear, then move to the left side by first moving the left foot and then the right. At the same time, strike to the left side with the left back fist to an attacker's face. The stance is still *Shikodachi.*

See Figs. 141a and b. This is the same technique photographed from the front.

continued on page 70

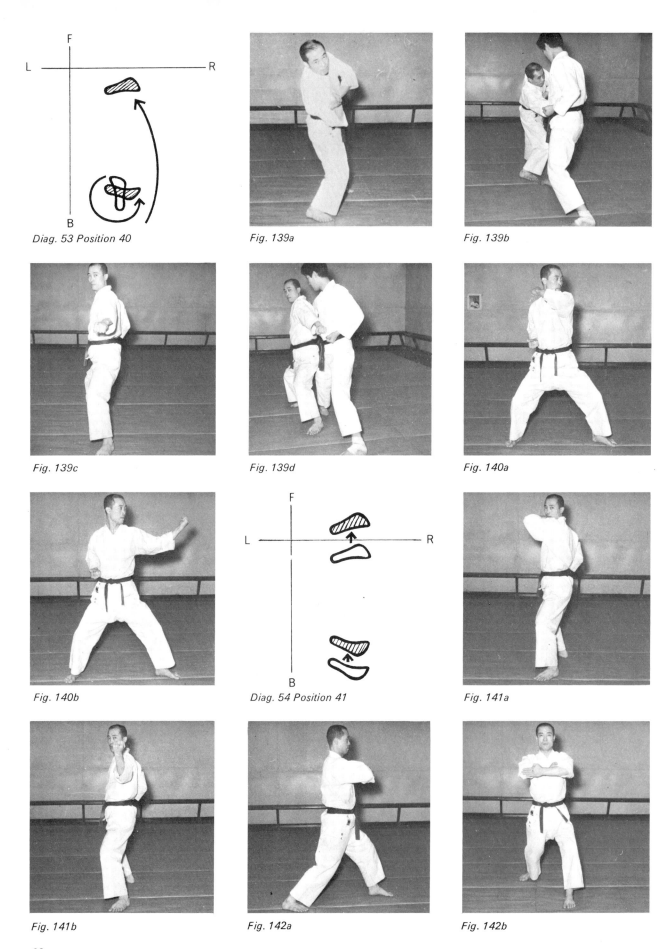

Diag. 53 Position 40

Fig. 139a

Fig. 139b

Fig. 139c

Fig. 139d

Fig. 140a

Fig. 140b

Diag. 54 Position 41

Fig. 141a

Fig. 141b

Fig. 142a

Fig. 142b

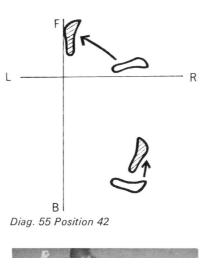

Diag. 55 Position 42

Fig. 143a

Fig. 143b

Fig. 143c

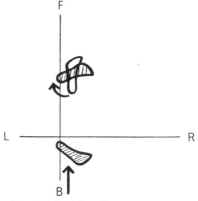

Diag. 56 Position 43

Fig. 144a

Fig. 144b

Fig. 144c

See Figs. 142a and b, and Diagram 55. Move the left foot slightly forward and to the left and bring up the right foot slightly. At the same time, twist the hips and strike the left palm with the right elbow punch.

See Figs. 143a, b, and c, and Diagram 56. Against an attack from behind, twist the hips to the right and at the same time bring the right foot up to the left leaving a distance of one shoulder width between the feet. At the same time, block the attacker's punch with right bottom fist and raise the left arm as shown, keeping the body at right angles to the attack.

See Figs. 144a, b, and c, and Diagram 57. The left foot moves across the front of the right foot and the body turns 180° to the right. Twist the hips strongly and at the same time the left arm moves in a wide arc and blocks a front kick attack. The back of the hand faces downwards. The right hand moves up into position as shown. The stance is *Shikodachi.*

Note 1. The left block and the right arm should be moved at the same speed and strength.

Note 2. Keep the body straight and facing front.

See Figs. 145a and b. The right arm moves down in an arc and blocks with bottom fist under the left arm as shown.

See Figs. 146a and b. Open the hands, keeping the thumbs bent, lift upwards together, and twist from the wrist. Stance is still *Shikodachi.* Keep the hips down.

See Figs. 147a and b, and Diagram 58. On an attack from the left, the left leg moves across the right leg and the body turns to the right 270° into *Junzuki* stance, the hands do not move.

See Figs. 148a and b. The hands are pulled quickly down and clenched, stopping with the elbows into the body and the forearms straight out as shown. This is a bottom fist block.

See Figs. 149, 150a, b, 151a, b, 152a, b, and Diagram 59. From this position move forward into right flying kick and when the feet touch the floor, strike the attacker's face with back fist.

Note. For the flying kick, jump up from the front foot and lift the rear knee as high as possible; during the jump lift the front knee as high as possible and kick and snap back. After the kick maintain a good balance by keeping the body slightly forward from the waist. After the kick the stance is *Junzuki.* At the same time as the back fist strikes, the left hand is pulled back to the hips.

See Figs. 153 and 154a, b, and Diagram 60. Take the left leg across the right leg to the right, turn the body to the right 180°. Bend the knees as shown; at the same time the right hand moves down into position and the left hand moves forward under the right hand as shown, with the back of the hand downwards.

Note 1. See Fig. 155 for the incorrect stance—the body should be more upright and the legs bent more.

See Fig. 156. This technique follows an attack from behind, as the body turns and the knees bend, so the attacker's punch goes over the defender's head and his hands move down and go inside the attacker's legs.

See Figs. 157a and b, 158. The legs are straightened, the body upright and the arms are quickly lifted each side of the head.

Note 1. When this technique is done quickly the attacker is thrown.

Note 2. During this movement the shoulders must be relaxed all the time.

Note 3. The arms must be kept in a straight line at the back of the head and not at the front.

continued on page 74

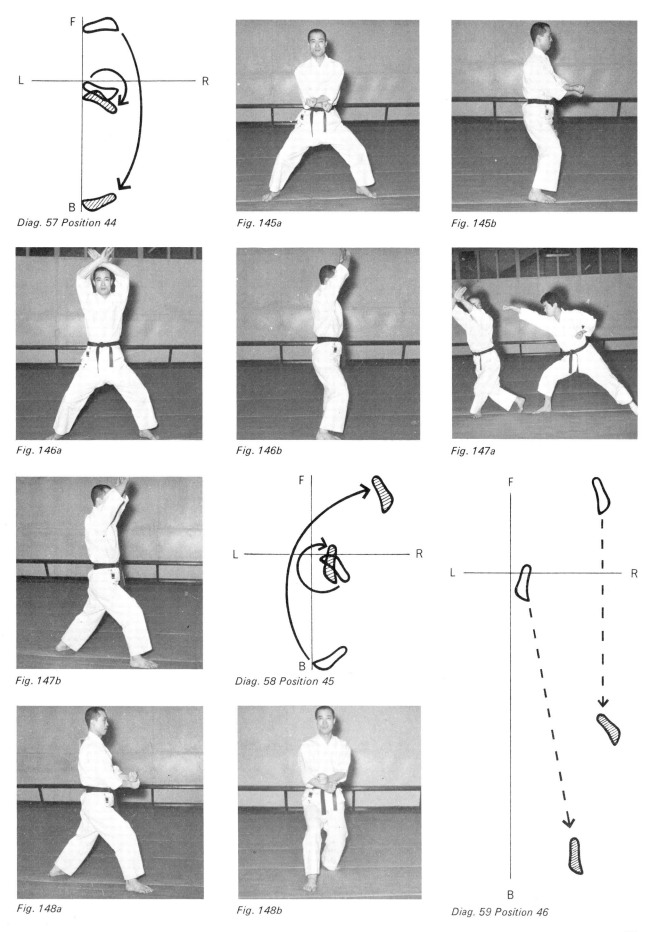

Diag. 57 Position 44

Fig. 145a

Fig. 145b

Fig. 146a

Fig. 146b

Fig. 147a

Fig. 147b

Diag. 58 Position 45

Fig. 148a

Fig. 148b

Diag. 59 Position 46

Fig. 149

Fig. 150a

Fig. 150b

Fig. 151a

Fig. 151b

Fig. 152a

Fig. 152b

Fig. 153

Fig. 154a

Fig. 154b

Diag. 60 Position 47

Fig. 155   Wrong View

Fig. 156

Fig. 157a

Fig. 157b

Fig. 158

Diag. 61a Position 48 (i)

Diag. 61b Position 48 (ii)

Note 4. The palms of the hands must face in to the head.

Note 5. The feet are a little wider apart than the shoulders. *See Diagrams 61a and b, and Fig. 84.* Pull the right foot in a little and at the same time bring the arms down as Fig. 84, left hand over the right. Next bring the left foot up halfway, then bring up the right foot together and the hands to the sides.

7 BASIC SPARRING & SEMI-FREE SPARRING

1. Basic Sparring (Kihon Gumite)

Basic sparring is a method of practising with an opponent, designed to develop defensive technique. In it you are kicked or punched on pre-arranged points. By this method, you gain experience in distancing and timing, which cannot be practised in individual training.

This system of sparring was introduced by the instructor Hironori Otsuka, the founder of the Wado school, after intensive training and study. It is designed very practically, in order that you may attain the greatest effect with the minimum of strength, without wasting any effort.

These techniques are extremely valuable. The more you practise, the more you will come to understand their immeasurable subtlety : they are as profound as Lao Tsue's saying, 'Softness controls strength.'

However, they are rather difficult for beginners, so I want you to practise them when you have read carefully what follows, and have understood the meaning of the techniques involved.

2. Semi-free Sparring (Ohyo Gumite)

Semi-free sparring is a method of practising techniques applicable to free sparring which I devised myself on the basis of my match-experience. Essential points which you must practise with care both in basic and in semi-free sparring are :

(a) *Distancing (Maai)*

Distancing means always keeping the proper distance, neither too far apart nor too near. This is absolutely essential in free sparring and in matches.

When two opponents are so close that their hands, held in the ready position are nearly touching, as shown later in Fig. 161b, they are incorrectly distanced, being too close. In such a case you can be easily surprised by a front kick, by having your hand grasped, or being punched by your opponent, who need not even shift his body.

On the other hand, if your distance apart is too great, you cannot reach your opponent in one pace, and so he will have no difficulty in avoiding your attack.

The proper distance, therefore, is to be near enough to knock down the opponent by a half-step forward with the leading foot from the ready position, but far enough away to allow for manoeuvre and body-shifting.

(b) *Body-shifting in Defence*

As the attacking points and the direction and method of attack are prearranged, as a defender one is liable to retreat before the opponent actually attacks. One is also liable to take a passive attitude in retreating when the opponent advances from his ready position. But it is essential for the defender that he should always have firmly fixed in his mind the intention of attacking, of taking advantage of the other's unguarded moments, even while withdrawing. After making a block one must be full of spirit and vitality for an immediate counter-attack. By practising these exercises constantly and properly, one develops as reflex actions the movements from defence to attack, to be used in free sparring and matches.

When a beginner withdraws, he is apt to retreat in the same direction as the opponent's blow; for example, if he shifts his body to the left, he retreats to the left. But it is illogical to do so. If you retreat in a slightly different direction, and entice your opponent on, it is easier to ward off the next attack.

In body-shifting, beginners who shift only their feet and block only with their hands will lose their balance. It is important for both attacker and defender to shift the weight of the body as well as the feet.

(c) *Seriousness of Purpose*

An attacker must always attack in earnest, with fighting spirit, really intending to knock down his opponent.

Practice must be performed in deadly earnest and seriousness. There should be no compromise. As long as beginners make an attack or a block thinking of it as mere exercise, they cannot learn the techniques properly.

First practise the actual techniques of attacking and blocking thoroughly until you have mastered them, and then always practise as if you were actually fighting.

If your opponent blocks you half-heartedly, strike at him hard, so that he learns that a defender should not be off his guard for a moment. It is only by such serious training that one can acquire the power and technique which enable one to take part in free-sparring and matches.

(d) *Zanshin*

Zanshin means keeping your mind alert. For example, if you knock your opponent down in a direct attack, you must not for a moment relax your attention. You must be always prepared to meet his next attack or an unexpected counter-attack.

There is a story which gives an example of Zanshin. Once there was an expert in Japanese fencing named Yoshioka Kenpo. One day he went mad and wounded many samurai. So nobody wanted to fight with him, until another samurai, well known for his skill in fencing, came along. He approached Yoshioka and fought with him. In the course of the fight it happened that Yoshioka stumbled on a stone and fell. Any ordinary man would have struck at him from above on such an occasion. However, this samurai said to him, 'I won't strike a man who has fallen. Stand up quickly.' The moment that Yoshioka stood up, his opponent stepped in and cut at him with his sword.

The samurai refrained from striking Yoshioka while he was on the ground because he knew that Yoshioka excelled in the move called Tsubamegoeshi ('Swallow's turn'), a technique in which one strikes upward from below after one has fallen. At that moment Yoshioka was indeed ready to strike at him, using Tsubamegoeshi. But unexpectedly the other did not attack him, but simply told him to stand up. This distracted his attention for a second, whereupon the other struck at him. This shows that Yoshioka neglected Zanshin and the other did not.

(e) *The Point to Keep your Eyes On*

Miyamoto Musashi, an expert in Kendo (Japanese fencing) says, 'Watch your opponent as if you were looking at a remote object.' This means that you must watch the whole of his body, not only his eyes.

It is essential that you should keep your eyes on your opponent, not only when both of you are standing face to face, but also when you are blocking or when you are standing apart. It is also important to remember 'Zanshin', to keep your mind alert.

8 KIHON GUMITE

BASIC SPARRING

See Figs. 159, 160, 161a, b, c, and d.

As already stressed, it is very important to ensure the correct distance between opponents. The method of finding the correct distance and beginning the various techniques is as follows: First the opponents bow. When the bow starts, sparring is considered to have begun so, with purpose and full of spirit, the contestants bow their heads slightly, always watching the other's eyes and never looking down or being otherwise off guard. *See Figs. 159 and 160.* Then A moves half a step forward, B withdraws half a step. The distance is called Maai. This distance is neither too far apart nor too close. *See Fig. 161a.* The distance is too close if one opponent can stretch his arm, grasp the other's hands, and throw or kick. *See Figs. 161b, c, and d.* If it is possible to punch in this position without moving, it is also too close. On the other hand, the distance is too far if, from the ready position, one is unable to reach one's opponent with a punch after moving forward half a step. From the correct distance a punch from the initial position cannot reach its target, but can if half a step forward is taken.

Note. The ready position is right stance.

Kihon Gumite No. 1 (*See Figs. 159–165 and Diagram 62.*)

Both A and B in right stance. A moves forward half a step with right and left foot and, with his body leaning forward, punches at the face of B with his right hand. B moves his left and right foot to the left, twisting his body to the left at the same time. *See Fig. 162.* He drops his hips a little and in the stance *Shikodachi,** as the illustrations show, blocks A's right-hand punch by bringing his own right hand up to the side of his right ear.

Note 1. If B moves too far to the left he cannot counter-attack, so it is important for him to attack and block with the minimum amount of movement.

Note 2. B must step back obliquely to the left, not straight back.

Note 3. B must not stop A's punch but must block it by letting it go past.

Note 4. B twists his body to the left and positions it at 45°.

Note 5. The weight is equally balanced on both feet. Both A and B must keep their elbows well into the sides. *See Figs. 163a, b, and c.*

*Shikodachi

In Japanese wrestling *Sumo,* the wrestlers raise their legs and stamp as a preparatory exercise before fighting. This stamping technique is called *Shiko-o-fumi.* The leg position used is the same as *Shikodachi* (*dachi* means stance). As Diagram 63 shows, the stance is with the toes outwards and the knees bent, the weight being evenly balanced between each foot.

Fig. 159

Fig. 160

continued on page 80

Fig. 161a

Fig. 161b

Fig, 161c

F

L   R

Diag. 62

B

Fig. 161d

Fig. 162

Fig. 163a

Fig. 163b

F

L – – – – – – – R

Diag. 63

B

Fig. 163c

Fig. 164a

Fig. 164b

Fig. 164c

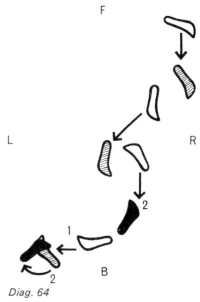

F

L   R

B

Diag. 64

Fig. 165a

Fig. 165b

Fig. 165c

Fig. 166

Fig. 167a

Fig. 167b

Fig. 167c   Wrong View

Fig. 168

A then slides forward to the right and punches at B's right ribs with his left reverse punch. B immediately moves his left foot to the left and, with his body also moving to the left, avoids A's punch by twisting his hips to the right. The punch is blocked to the side with B's right hand and at the same time he punches upwards to the stomach with his left hand. *See Figs. 164a, b, c, and 165a, b, c, and Diagram 64.*

Note 1. It is important for B to avoid the punch by shifting his body to the left instead of just blocking with his hand.

Note 2. When B blocks, his knees and his toes must be tensed inwards, and he must put most of his weight on his left foot. He must be careful not to withdraw his right foot too far backwards.

Note 3. He must keep his back straight, watch A all the time and *never* look down.

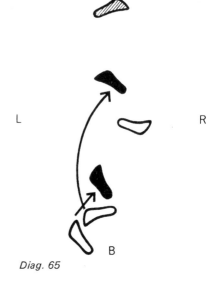

Diag. 65

Kihon Gumite No. 2 (*See Figs. 166–170.*)

The first attack and block are the same as *Kihon Gumite* No. 1. Then A, sliding his left foot in half a step, kicks at B's right ribs with right Sokuto. B withdraws his left foot and then right foot obliquely to the left, at the same time twisting his hips to the left. Making full use of this twist he blocks A's Sokuto with his right hand from above to the right. (*See Figs. 167a and b.*)

Note 1. B must keep his hips down and must block by twisting his hips as fully as possible.

Note 2. He must not withdraw straight back but obliquely to the right.

Note 3. When he blocks, B must keep his back straight and watch A all the time. If he only pulls back his hips and leaves the other part of his body leaning forwards, he will lose his balance. *See Fig. 167c.* This is incorrect.

Note 4. When B pulls back his right knee he must keep it close to his left knee.

Then B lowers his hands to his left side and makes his right hand into Haito and his left hand into Teisho (*see Fig. 168*). He then moves his right foot forwards to the middle of A's legs with his toes inwards, and sliding his left foot forwards at the same time, he strikes upwards at A's right ribs with his right Haito; he also strikes at the kidneys with his left Teisho, twisting his hips at the same time. (*See Figs. 169a and b.*)

Note 1. B must keep his body close to A's, *not* as in Fig. 169c.

Note 2. B must ensure that he steps in the middle of A's feet sufficiently. Then he must move into, and press against, A with his body. (*See Figs. 169a and b, and Diagram 65.*)

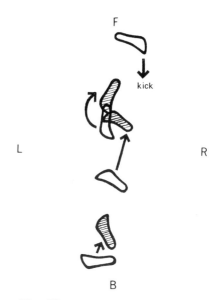

Diag. 66

See Figs. 170a, b, and c. These photographs show how the two opponents must separate. They must be watchful and quick as the illustrations indicate. This is called 'Zanshin'. Although this movement is not always the same every time, it must invariably be carried out quickly and with good spirit—keeping a good balance and being ready to attack or block at any moment.

Kihon Gumite No. 3 (*See Figs. 171, 172 and Diagram 66.*)

The first attack and block are the same as *Kihon Gumite* Nos. 1 and 2. After which A, as Diagram 66 shows, withdraws his front foot slightly and tries to kick at B's right ribs with his left foot. (*See Figs. 171a, b, and c.*) As soon as he raises his foot B, moving his right foot inward slightly to the inside of A's right foot, leans his body forward and strikes at the inside of A's thigh with the left fist. At the same time, he punches upwards at A's stomach with his right hand. (*See Figs. 172a, b, and c.*)

Fig. 169a

Fig. 169b

Fig. 169c Wrong View

Fig. 170a

Fig. 170b

Fig. 170c

Fig. 171a

Fig. 171b

Fig. 171c

Fig. 172a

Fig. 172b

Fig. 172c

Note 1. B must bend his right knee inwards when he moves it forwards.

Note 2. B must attack with his right and left hand at the same time. When he strikes, he twists his hips to the left. This is because when he punches at A's right side with his left hand, his body tends to twist to the right.

Note 3. B puts his head against A's right chest.

Note 4. When he strikes, B must keep his right elbow in to the side and not let if lift, in order to protect his ribs.

Note 5. If B's timing is late he will be kicked; therefore, as soon as A is about to kick, B must move quickly into the position of Fig. 172.

Kihon Gumite No. 4 (*See Figs. 173–177 and Diagrams 67 and 68.*)

A is in left stance and B is in right stance. A slides forward and punches at the face with his left hand. B blocks the blow in the same way as *Kihon Gumite* Nos. 1, 2, and 3. Then A slides forward to the right, as in Diagram 67, and punches at the face with a right reverse punch, twisting his hips (*Figs. 173a, b, c*). B, withdrawing first his left foot and then his right foot obliquely to the left, opens his left hand and blocks across the face and backwards, his hand moving from A's right elbow to his wrist (*Figs. 174a, b*). B's wrist must be twisted during this sweeping block.

Note 1. B must keep his face and upper body leaning backwards because he cannot block a strong punch if he only uses a hand movement (*Fig. 175*).

Note 2. B must block from the front to the back, sweeping A's punch aside. After the block, B's left hand must be besides his right ear. *See Fig. 176.*

Note 3. B must bend his left knee, pull back his right foot and raise the heel close to his left foot.

Note 4. B must not move straight back but must move obliquely to the left. B's waist must be twisted to the right. Then, making use of the reaction and leaning his upper body backwards, he moves forward and breaks A's balance by pushing his elbow forward to the right with his left knifehand; at the same time he strikes at A's armpit with his right hand middle finger one knuckle fore fist. *See Figs. 177a and b.*

Note 1. B's right foot must be turned slightly inward and his knees must also be tensed inwards.

Note 2. B must bend forward from the waist, pushing his face against A's body.

Note 3. To break A's balance it is necessary to push his right arm.

Kihon Gumite No. 5 (*See Figs. 178–187 and Diagram 69.*)

The first block is the same as *Kihon Gumite* No. 4. Then A slides forward also as for No. 4, and punches at the lower part of B's right ribs with his right hand. B, withdrawing his left foot half a step, lowers his hips and blocks down with the small finger side of his right wrist. *See Figs. 178a and b.*

B then blocks A's right hand to the left and, sliding forward with his right and left foot, hooks A's nose upwards with his right, bent forefinger. *See Figs. 179a and b.*

Once again, B slides forwards slightly and, pulling A's right hand with his left hand, he punches A's right ribs with his right elbow in a sideways movement. *See Figs. 180a and b.* Then B pulls back his right foot up to his left and grasps A's right arm, as Diagram 70, and throws him by twisting his arm clockwise. *See Figs. 181, 182, 183, 184a and b.*

Note 1. In throwing, B pulls A's hand, as if describing a circle with A's

F

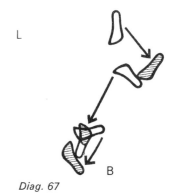
L   R

Diag. 67

F

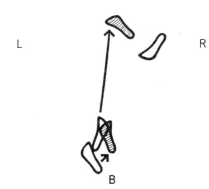
L   R

B

Diag. 68

F

L   R

B

Diag. 69

Fig. 173a

Fig. 173b

Fig. 173c

Fig. 174a

Fig. 174b

Fig. 175   Wrong View

Fig. 176

Fig. 177a

Fig. 177b

Fig. 178a

Fig. 178b

Fig. 179a

Fig. 179b

Fig. 180a

Fig. 180b

Diag. 70

Fig. 181

Fig. 182

Fig. 183

Fig. 184a

Fig. 184b

Diag. 71

Fig. 185a

Fig. 185b

Fig. 186a

Fig. 186b

Fig. 187

Fig. 188a

right shoulder as the centre. In order to keep A's arm straight, B twists it outward during the movement.

Note 2. When B holds A's hand, he steps slightly forward with his right foot and takes a long step backwards with his left, obliquely to the right. At the same time he twists his hips to the left, and throws A as he twists his hand to the outside. After throwing, B steps against A's right shoulder, holding his hand and twisting it to the outside as Diagram 71 shows. B then kneels on A's right elbow to the left. A's right hand being pulled above his head as he lays on the ground. *See Figs. 185a and b.* Then, pressing A's elbow, B strikes at the face with his right fore fist. *See Figs. 186a and b, 187.*

Kihon Gumite No. 6 (*See Figs. 188–191.*)

The first stance, attack, and block are the same as *Kihon Gumite* Nos. 4. and 5. *See Figs. 188a and b.* Then A, sliding forward half a step with his right foot, kicks with the left foot edge to B's right ribs. B blocks in the same way as *Kihon Gumite* No. 2. *See Figs. 189a and b.* A then steps forward with the left kicking foot, punches to the face with right fore fist reverse punch. Against this punch, B sways back slightly and at the same time moves his left foot to the left. *See Fig. 190.* Twisting his hips to the right and making full use of the hip twist, B opens his hand and blocks with the back of it. This block moves backwards and to the right obliquely. At the same time B punches upwards to the neck with his left hand. *See Fig. 191.*

Note. The block of the kick is the same as in *Kihon Gumite* No. 2 and the shift of the body and feet before the last right reverse punch, is the same as the last block in *Kihon Gumite* No. 1.

Kihon Gumite No. 7 (*See Figs. 192–193 and Diagram 72.*)

The first stance and attack is the same as in *Kihon Gumite* No. 6. *See Figs. 192a and b.* Then A withdraws slightly with his left foot and kicks with a right roundhouse kick to the stomach. Before the kick is completed, as Diagram 72 shows, B twists his body to the left and with his right foot turned slightly inwards, leans forward, opens his hand and strikes at the chin with his knifehand. His back foot is moved to the right, as in Diagram 72, and his hips are twisted to the right.

Note 1. These movements—stepping forward, hip twisting, striking at the chin with knife hand, and moving the left hand in front of the chest to block the kick—must be carried out quickly and simultaneously.

Note 2. It is essential that the timing for this technique should be perfect, therefore all the various exercises which give practice in timing should be constantly repeated.

Note 3. When B steps forward, he must step straight and not to the side. Also B must bump his body against A's and lean forward. At the same time, he avoids the roundhouse kick by moving his foot to the right. *See Figs. 193a, b, c, and d.*

Kihon Gumite No. 8 (*See Figs. 194–199.*)

Both A and B are in right stance. Sliding forward with his right foot A punches at B's chest with his right fore fist. B, as in Diagram 73, slightly withdraws his right and left foot obliquely to the right, and with his hips swivelling to the left, twists his right fist inward so that the back of the hand faces outward. He then brings up his right elbow round to the left, and deflects A's punch to the left with a quick strike of the elbow. *See Figs. 194a and b.*

Note 1. B must be careful that his left foot is not turned outward too

continued on page 89

Fig. 188b

Fig. 189a

Fig. 189b

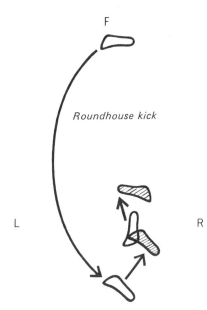

F

Roundhouse kick

L

R

B

Diag. 72

Fig. 190

Fig. 191

Fig. 192a

Fig. 192b

Fig. 193a

Fig. 193b

Fig. 193c

Fig. 193d

Fig. 194a

Fig. 194b

Diag. 73

Fig. 195

Diag. 74

Fig. 196a

Fig. 196b

Fig. 196c

Diag. 75

Fig. 197a

Fig. 197b

Fig. 198a

Fig. 198b

Fig. 199a

Fig. 199b

Fig. 199c

Fig. 200a

Fig. 200b

Fig. 200c

Fig. 201a

Fig. 201b

Diag. 76

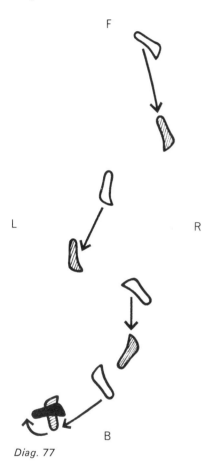

Diag. 77

Fig. 202a

much, otherwise, when he twists his hips he may lose his balance. *See Diagram 73.*

Note 2. B's hips must be lowered slightly. *See Fig. 195.*

A slides forward and punches with left reverse punch. As in Diagram 74, B withdraws his left foot obliquely to the left and blocks the punch by raising his elbow. His head must not lean backwards, but he must draw in his neck to the front and keep his eyes on A all the time. *See Figs. 196a, b, and c.*

Then B, as in Diagram 75, moves his right and left foot forward and to the left, twists his hips to the left and leans his body forward from the waist, to the right. At the same time he punches downward to A's thigh with his right fore fist.

Note. B must strike the thigh as hard as possible, helped by the forward motion of his body. *See Figs. 197a and b.*

B then slides slightly forward and strikes at A's stomach with his right elbow in a sideways movement. The stance is *Shikodachi.* (*See Diagram 76.*)

Note 1. B must keep his back straight, with his weight distributed evenly in the centre.

Note 2. The elbow strike is stronger if the right hand is pressed on the left. *See Figs. 198a and b.*

B twists the inside of A's knee with the inside of his own right knee; at the same time, opening both hands, he presses A's right wrist with them from above with a twisting movement. As soon as A loses his balance, B withdraws quickly. This technique demonstrates the way to break an opponents balance by first pressing then quickly moving back.

Note. Both of B's elbows must be tensed inwards and not lifted during the pressing motion. *See Figs. 199a, b, and c.*

Kihon Gumite No. 9 (*See Figs. 200 and 201.*)

The first stance and block are the same as for *Kihon Gumite* No. 8. A, sliding forward, punches at the chest above B's blocking arm. B, as in Diagram 77, moves his left foot to the side, turning his body sideways, opens his hand, and blocks the punch backwards and to the right (*Figs. 200a, b, c*). This is done obliquely with his right backhand, with the wrist bending in a snapping movement. At the same time he punches upwards with his left hand, as A is leaning forward.

Note 1. The moving of B's feet and body is the same as in the last techniques of *Kihon Gumite* Nos. 1 and 6.

Note 2. As B is punched on his right chest, it is important that he twists his body to the right obliquely backwards from his right shoulder. It is more important to twist the body away from the punch than to block with the hand, as already emphasized. *See Figs. 201a and b.*

Kihon Gumite No. 10 (*See Figs. 202–209.*)

Both are in right stance. A, sliding forward, punches at B's face with his right fore fist. B withdraws slightly as in *Kihon Gumite* Nos. 8 and 9 and moves obliquely to the right, blocking A's right arm from above with a right knifehand. B's left hand is placed against his chest in the ready position. *See Figs. 202a and b.* A slides forward obliquely to the right and punches at the face with his left reverse punch. B, leaning his face and upper body slightly forward to the left (*see Figs. 203a, b, and c*), sweeps this punch backwards obliquely to the right, with the thumb side of his right wrist. As in Diagram 78, he then moves forward with the feet turned inwards, and presses A's left hand from above, so that his right hand cannot punch.

continued on page 92

Fig. 202b

Fig. 203a

Fig. 203b

F

L

R

B

Diag. 78

Fig. 203c

Fig. 204a

Fig. 204b

Fig. 205a

Fig. 205b

Fig. 206a

Fig. 206b

Fig. 206c

Diag. 79

Fig. 207a

Fig. 207b

Fig. 208a

Fig. 208b

Diag. 80

Fig. 209a

Fig. 209b

Note 1. When B blocks with his right hand, it must be lifted to the right side of his face beside his right ear.

Note 2. B's face must be kept close to A's right chest. *See Figs. 204a and b.*

Then, quickly grasping A's collar with his right hand, B pushes up A's chin (*see Figs. 205a and b*) and, moving his right foot to the right, pushes up his right hand which is grasping A's collar. This causes A's body to be pulled forward. At once B open his left hand and strikes upward at A's groin with his backhand.

Note. It is important that B moves his right foot to the side and twists his hips to the right while pulling upwards. *See Figs. 206a, b, and c.*

The punch to A's body causes him to lose his balance, so B moves his left foot to the side (*see Diagram 79*) of A's left foot, and between his two feet. B then turns his body completely from the right and throws A on to his back.

Note 1. B pulls the hand which is grasping A's collar, close to his side so that A's body is close to his back.

Note 2. B stretches his left hand backwards and puts it on A's left thigh. *See Figs. 207a and b.* Then, dropping his right hand forward and down, and pushing up his left hand which is on A's thigh, he withdraws his right foot, bends his upper body quickly forward and throws A. *See Figs. 208a and b, and Diagram 80.* After being thrown, A get up immediately, pulling in his feet. *See Figs. 209a and b.*

Note. B must keep his eyes upon A and have 'Zanshin'. (*See section on 'Zanshin' in Chapter 7.*)

It is very important to practise all these *Kihon Gumite* techniques correctly, and quickly.

Fig. 210

9 OHYO GUMITE
SEMI-FREE SPARRING

Fig. 211a

Fig. 211b

Fig. 211c

Ohyo Gumite No. 1 (*See Figs. 210–215.*)

This technique is mainly used to practise the Foot Sweep. First A and B adopt the stance shown in Fig. 210. Then A takes one step forward and punches at B's face. The blow is blocked, so A punches once more, with a left reverse punch to B's ribs. *See Figs. 211a, b, c, 212a, b, c.*

Note 1. A must move forward very quickly in order to strengthen his punch by the speed of the movement.

Note 2. When punching the face and ribs, A must withdraw his hands very quickly, ready for the next move. If he is too slow then B may grab his hands, also his focus will be bad and he will not be in a correct position for the next movement. *See Fig. 213a.* A sweeps his left foot forward as shown by the dotted line, moving B's front foot to A's right. The contact is made with the sole of A's foot against B's ankle. He not only uses his foot but also twists his body at the waist. At the same time his stance changes; the sweeping foot moves back to the left and slightly forward and A punches to the ribs with a right reverse punch. If the foot sweep is done correctly B's balance will be broken. After the reverse punch the hand must be quickly withdrawn. *See Figs. 213a, b, c, 214a, b, c.* When the reverse punch is completed A can take his left foot a little further to the left and kick to B's stomach or face with a right roundhouse kick. *See Fig. 215.*

Ohyo Gumite No. 2 (*See Figs. 216–222.*)

A and B adopt opposite stances (*Fig. 216*). This technique is mainly to practise the foot hook intended to break the opponent's balance. A moves his right foot slightly and punches at B's face with his left hand. B blocks his punch to the right with his left hand. *See Figs. 217a and b.* A then moves his left rear foot forward half a step and slides his right foot behind B's left front foot. A's upper body stays in the same position. He then moves his foot with his left hip forward. *See Figs. 218a and b.* A sweeps the heels of B's front foot with the part of his foot at the base of the big toe on his right foot, pulling the foot to his rear.

Note 1. A must sweep backwards and towards his own left foot, not to the side.

Note 2. A must sweep the lower part of B's foot.

Note 3. If the body leans forwards slightly the hook will be very strong. *See Figs. 219a, b, and c.*

The hooking foot is moved forward and, twisting right at the waist, A punches B's left ribs with a left reverse punch. If B is too close, the punch can be made with the elbow or delivered by means of a ridgehand to the face or stomach. Sometimes a throw can be made without punching in the same way as *Ohyo Gumite* No. 3. *See Figs. 220a, b, 221a, b, 222a, b.*

continued on page 99

Fig. 212a

Fig. 212b

Fig. 212c

Fig. 213a

Fig. 213b

Fig. 213c

Fig. 214a

Fig. 214b

Fig. 214c

Fig. 215

Fig. 216

Fig. 217a

94

Fig. 217b

Fig. 218a

Fig. 218b

Fig. 219a

Fig. 219b

Fig. 219c

Fig. 220a

Fig. 220b

Fig. 221b

Fig. 222a

Fig. 222b

Fig. 223

Fig. 224a

Fig. 224b

Fig. 225a

Fig. 225b

Fig. 226

Fig. 227a

Fig. 227b

Fig. 228a

Fig. 228b

Fig. 229

Fig. 230

Fig. 231

Fig. 232

Fig. 233a

Fig. 233b

Fig. 233c

Fig. 234a

Fig. 234b

Fig. 234c

Fig. 235a

Fig. 235b

Ohyo Gumite No. 3 (*See Figs. 223, 224a, b, 225a, b, 226, 227a, b, 228a, b, 229, 230.*)

This is a throwing technique. A is in right stance and B is in left stance. B steps forward and punches to A's face with his right hand, following with a left-hand punch to the stomach. A steps back and sways the upper part of his body backwards. A then moves forwards with his left and right foot, keeping the same stance, and punches B's face with his left hand. B bends forward from the waist obliquely to the left and allows the punch to go over the top. B then brings up his right hand under A's chin and puts his left hand behind A's left knee, with the hand twisted anti-clockwise and the thumb downward. B then quickly slides forward a little and, twisting his hips to the right and straightening his legs, throws A to the rear. During the throw, B's body leans backwards slightly. The right hand moves down in an arc and the left hand moves up in an arc simultaneously. After the throw, B strikes A's face with a backhand.

Note 1. When B attacks he must be sure to move his front foot slightly to the right, because when A attacks he may stamp on B's foot.

Note 2. See Fig. 231. This is incorrect. B's body must be closer to A in order to throw.

Ohyo Gumite No. 4 (*See Figs. 232–239.*)

This is a sequence of techniques: back fist, reverse punch and knee kick, and downward elbow strike. A moves his right foot slightly forward and strikes at the face with right back fist, then withdraws his hand quickly. He then takes one step forward with his left foot, holds B's right hand with his left hand and punches to the stomach with a right reverse punch.

Note 1. When punching with back fist the defender steps forward with his left foot and also delivers a right reverse punch. These movements have to be done in quick succession.

Note 2. It is important when punching with back fist to extend the arm to the full. *See Figs. 232, 233a, b, c, 234a, b, c, 235a, b, c, 236a, b, c*. A reaches out with his right arm to grasp the back of B's collar and with his left hand grips B's right sleeve. He then pulls downward with his arms and kicks upwards with his right knee. He follows up by lowering this foot in front of B and at the same time striking the back of B's neck with a right elbow punch. *See Figs. 237, 238a, b, c, 239a, b, c*.

Ohyo Gumite No. 5 (*See Figs. 240–251.*)

This technique demonstrates a method of blocking a kick. Moving one step forward with his right foot, A pulls back his left hand quickly and delivers a reverse punch with it. B steps back with his left foot, twisting his hip, and blocks to the left with his right forearm. *See Figs. 240, 241a, b, and c*. A slides forward half a step with his left foot, then front kicks with his right foot. B steps back with his right foot and sweeps the kick with his left hand. As A loses his balance B strikes A in the stomach with a right ridgehand, his hand describing a wide arc. B then turns his hand and strikes the right side of A's face with a back fist. *See Figs. 242a, b, c, 243, 244a, b, 245a, b, 246a, b, c, 247a, b, c*.

Note 1. When A slides forwards, B goes straight back with his right foot. When A kicks B slides his left foot to the left, straightens his left arm to the left and, opening the hand, twists his waist to the right. Shifting his weight to the left, he sweeps A's kicking leg to the right. This block can also be made with the hand clenched but contact is always made with the palm heel of the hand.

continued on page 104

Fig. 235c

Fig. 236a

Fig. 236b

Fig. 236c

Fig. 237

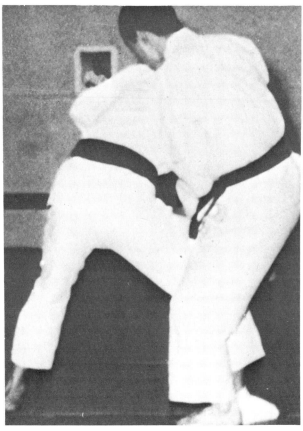

Fig. 238a

Fig. 238b

Fig. 238c

Fig. 239a

Fig. 239b

Fig. 239c

Fig. 240

Fig. 241a

Fig. 241b

Fig. 241c

Fig. 242a

Fig. 242b

Fig. 242c

102

Fig. 243

Fig. 244a

Fig. 244b

Fig. 245a

Fig. 245b

Fig. 246a

Fig. 246b

Fig. 246c

Fig. 247a

Fig. 247b

Fig. 247c

Fig. 248a

Fig. 248b

Fig. 248c

Fig. 249a

Note 2. When B blocks the kick he must make full use of the hip twist and not just use the arm movement. He must also keep his back straight, head up and put his weight on the right foot, maintaining a good balance, with his left foot just touching the ground.

B then grasps the back of A's collar with his left hand and turns his body to the left. With his right knee lowered he pulls down with his left hand. With his right hand he strikes A at the back of his right knee, so forcing him to the ground. *See Figs. 248a, b, c, 249a, b, c, 250a, b, c, 251a, b, c.*

Note 1. If B strikes the back of A's knee using only his hand it is difficult to break the balance, B must lower his waist and place his right knee behind A's right foot first.

Note 2. When he throws, B must move his left foot to the left side and twist his waist. If he throws without moving his left foot he cannot twist his waist. Also, A will drop on to his foot and probably hurt him.

After A is down, B must strike his face with a right knifehand. *See Fig. 251c.*

Fig. 249b

Ohyo Gumite No. 6 (*See Figs. 252–258.*)

This technique illustrates the hook and roundhouse kick. A slides forwards with his right foot and front kicks with his left foot, at the same time stepping forward and punching B's face with a right reverse punch. B steps back with his left foot, avoiding A's kick, and blocks the punch with his right hand. *See Figs. 252, 253a, b, 254a, b, 255a, b, c.* A then hooks B's right foot with his left foot in the same way as *Ohyo Gumite* No. 2. After hooking, A moves this foot slightly to the left and roundhouse kicks to the head with his right foot.

Note 1. When A roundhouse kicks. If A's supporting left leg is too close to B when he roundhouse kicks, it makes the move very difficult. Therefore, after hooking he must move his foot to the side to maintain the correct distance. *See Figs. 256a, b, c, 257a, b, c, 258a, b, c.*

Fig. 249c

Ohyo Gumite No. 7 (*See Figs. 259–265.*)

This technique shows how to block a front kick and throw from behind. Both men begin in left stance. A slides forwards with his left foot and punches with *Tobikomizuki*. He then slides his left foot forward once more and again punches with *Tobikomizuki* (left-hand double punch to the face). Against this attack B retreats with first his left foot then his right, blocking A's punches to the face with his left hand as in Figs. 259a and b. After blocking, B counter-attacks with a right front kick. (B must maintain good balance while retreating.) A then blocks the kick to the right, moving his left foot to the left in the same way as *Ohyo Gumite* No. 5. As B loses his balance A punches the lower ribs of B's

Fig. 250a

continued on page 111

Fig. 250b

Fig. 250c

Fig. 251a

Fig. 251b

Fig. 251c

Fig. 252

Fig. 253a

Fig. 253b

Fig. 254a

Fig. 254b

Fig. 255a

Fig. 255b

Fig. 255c

Fig. 256a

Fig. 256b

Fig. 256c

Fig. 257a

Fig. 257b

Fig. 257c

Fig. 258a

Fig. 258b

Fig. 258c

Fig. 259a

Fig. 259b

Fig. 260a

Fig. 260b

Fig. 260c

Fig. 261a

Fig. 261b

Fig. 261c

Fig. 262a

Fig. 262b

Fig. 262c

Fig. 263a

Fig. 263b

Fig. 263c

Fig. 264a

Fig. 264b

Fig. 264c

Fig. 265a

Fig. 265b

Fig. 266a

Fig. 266b

Fig. 267a

Fig. 267b

Fig. 267c

Fig. 268a

Fig. 268b

Fig. 268c

Fig. 269a

Fig. 269b

Fig. 269c

Fig. 270a

Fig. 270b

Fig. 270c

Fig. 271a

Fig. 271b

Fig. 271c

Fig. 272a

Fig. 272b

Fig. 272c

Fig. 273a

Fig. 273b   Fig. 273c

back with a right reverse punch. *See Figs. 259a, b, 260a, b, c, 261a, b, c.* A grasps the back of B's collar with his right hand and slides behind B. He then raises his right foot and stamp kicks the back of B's right knee with the edge of his foot. At the same time A pulls down with his right hand, forcing B to the ground.

Note 1. Unlike judo throws, it is important to stamp kick down on the knee joint sufficiently hard to break the balance. *See Figs. 262a, b, c, 263a, b, c, 264a, b, c, 265a, b.*

Ohyo Gumite No. 8 (*See Figs. 266a, b, 267a, b, c, 268a, b, c, 269a, b, c, 270a, b, c, 271a, b, c, 272a, b, c, 273a, b, c.*)

A is in left stance and B is in right stance. B moves his back foot slightly towards the front foot and hooks A's front foot towards him. A moves his foot back quickly into right stance. B then swings his left foot into *Ashi Barai* (foot sweep) against A's right foot. A quickly steps back with his right foot and B then steps to the right with his left side towards A, twisting his hips to the right. He turns and back kicks with his right foot to A's stomach. B is then facing backwards. After the kick, B twists his hips to the right, facing the front once more, and punches with his left hand to A's ribs.

Fig. 274a

Fig. 274b

Fig. 275a

Fig. 275b

Fig. 276a

Fig. 276b

Fig. 277a

Fig. 277b

Fig. 278a

10 DEFENCE AGAINST KNIFE ATTACK

In knife defence you must remember to move your body rather more than in fist fighting, to allow for the length of the knife.

I myself have had my hand cut about ten times in the course of hundreds of knife-defence demonstrations in Japan and abroad.

Beginners should not practise knife defence, as it requires a high degree of skill. You will only get hurt, without acquiring any additional basic techniques.

Knife defence is, however, one of the excellent arts of the Wado school. It clearly emphasizes the features of attacking with hands and feet which is unique in Karate, and adapts the techniques of Aiki.

We use a piece of wood for a knife until we have mastered the techniques.

When taking the part of attacker it is essential to strike directly at the object of your attack, either with the piece of wood or with the knife. You must attack without reservation, otherwise the defender will not take your attack seriously. He will then not only be unable to master the proper method of defence but will also get hurt.

When defending, you must be careful to be accurate when you are about to grasp your opponent's hand in order to throw him, for a miscalculation means that you will cut your hand on the blade.

KNIFE DEFENCE AGAINST THE THRUST

Knife Defence No. 1 (*See Figs. 274–281.*)

The attacker holds the knife in the left hand, withdraws the sheath, and holding the sheath over the head feints with it as though to stab the defender, in order to distract his attention. The knife is held tightly at the defender's left hip (*see Figs. 274a and b*) and while the defender's attention is on the hand holding the sheath, the attacker thrusts forward with the knife at the stomach, moving forward at the same time. The defender moves his left foot backwards and to the right, at the same time withdrawing his stomach, lifting his left hand and blocking the attacker's left wrist to the left side with the inside of his hand (turning the hand downwards). *See Figs. 275a and b.*

Note 1. It is important for the defender to keep his hips down during the block.

Now the defender turns the blocking hand upwards and grasps the attacker's wrist. He moves forward with the right foot, stretching his left arm and pushing the attacker's hand holding the knife to the left. As he does so he strikes the attacker's face with a right uraken (back fist).

Note 2. The defender must be careful to avoid the knife when he grasps the attacker's left hand.

Note 3. The defender must be careful when he grasps the attacker's wrist, to push the knifehand away sufficiently to avoid the blade. *See Figs. 276a and b*.

The defender holds up the attacker's left hand with his right hand underneath and kicks with left maegeri (front kick) to the stomach. *See Figs. 277a and b*. He then brings the kicking foot down beside the attacker's left foot and at the same time pushes the attacker's knifehand forward with both his hands. It is important to break the attacker's balance. *See Figs. 278a and b*. He then moves his right foot behind the attacker's left foot, twisting his body to the left and making a complete turn, which leaves him facing the same way as the attacker.

Note 1. When the defender makes a complete turn, he must continue holding the attacker's left wrist tightly.

Note 2. The defender must keep his body close to the attacker during the turn and move his right foot forward.

Note 3. When the defender stretches the attacker's arm forward, he must lift slightly upwards as though trying to pull the attacker's body up. *See Figs. 279a and b*.

The defender pulls down the attacker's left arm twisting the hand and dropping the hips. The attacker then goes over because his hand is being twisted against the joint. *See Figs. 280, 281a and b*.

Note 1. As the defender throws he must pull the attacker's arm down very quickly.

Note 2. The defender must twist the attacker's hand against the joint very strongly.

Note 3. When the defender throws, he must be careful to keep the knife clear of his thigh.

Knife Defence No. 2 *(See Figs. 282–288.)*

When the attacker thrusts for the stomach, the defender moves his left foot to the left, twists his body to the right and, pushing out his left hand to the right, blocks the knifehand. *See Figs. 282, 283a, b, c*.

Note. The defender must make sure that his hips are sufficiently twisted to the right to avoid the thrust. He must also ensure that his right hand is not too near the knife. *See Fig. 284*.

He then grasps the attacker's wrist with his right hand from above and pulls lightly. At the same time he strikes with his left open backhand to the ribs. *See Figs. 285a, b, c*. In the same way as Knife Defence No. 1 but on the opposite side, the defender twists the hand of the attacker and throws. *See Figs. 286a, b, c, 287a, b, c, 288a, b*.

Knife Defence No. 3 *(See Figs. 289–296.)*

When the attacker thrusts in the same way as No. 1, the defender steps backwards and to the left with his stomach withdrawn. He then blocks the thrust with his right hand. *See Figs. 289, 290a, b, 291a, b, c*. After which he pushes down the attacker's wrist with his left hand and strikes his face with a right backhand. *See Figs. 292a, b, c*. Then from underneath, the defender puts his right hand on the attacker's right hand, twists his own body to the left and throws the attacker by twisting his wrist. *See Figs. 293a, b, c, 294a, b, c, 295a, b, 296a, b, c*.

Note. The defender must keep the attacker's arm straight during the throw, by pulling downward and forwards as if drawing a circle, with the attacker's shoulder as the centre.

continued on page 120

Fig. 278b

Fig. 279a

Fig. 279b

Fig. 280

Fig. 281a

Fig. 281b

Fig. 282

Fig. 283a

Fig. 283b

Fig. 283c

Fig. 284

Fig. 285a

Fig. 285b

Fig. 285c

Fig. 286a

Fig. 286b

Fig. 286c

Fig. 287a

Fig. 287b

Fig. 287c

Fig. 288a

Fig. 288b

Fig. 289

Fig. 290a

Fig. 290b

Fig. 291a

Fig. 291b

Fig. 291c

Fig. 292a

Fig. 292b

Fig. 292c

Fig. 293a

Fig. 293b

Fig. 293c

Fig. 294a

Fig. 294b

Fig 294c

Fig. 295a

Fig. 295b

Fig. 296a

Fig. 296b

Fig. 296c

Fig. 297

Fig. 298

Fig. 299a

Fig. 299b

Fig. 300a

Fig. 300b

Fig. 301a

Fig. 301b

Fig. 302a

Fig. 302b

Fig. 303a

Fig. 303b

Knife Defence No. 4 (See Figs. 297–304.)

When the attacker thrusts for the stomach or stabs downwards (see Fig. 297) the defender goes down to the left and kicks with a right roundhouse kick.

Note. The defender must make sure that his body is down low enough. *See Figs. 298, 299a and b.*

Then he punches upwards at the attacker's stomach with his right fist and holds the attacker's right knee with his left hand. *See Figs. 300a and b.* After which, he brings his left foot up to the attacker's knee, opens both his hands and strikes simultaneously with right and left palm heel to the stomach and back. *See Figs. 301a and b.* The defender then straightens himself and with both palm heels strikes under the chin and the back of the neck with an upward movement. *See Figs. 302a and b.*

Note 1. The defender must be sure to strike straight upwards to the chin and back of the neck, and not out and in.

Note 2. The defender must put his right shoulder under the attacker's knife arm as though lifting him up and then pull his left foot backwards and to the right, twisting his body to the left and pushing the attacker backwards and down. *See Figs. 303a, b, 304.*

Fig. 304

Knife Defence No. 5 (See Figs. 305–310.)

When the attacker's thrust is very strong and the defender cannot block easily, he must step back (see Figs. 305a and b) and to the left. He then blocks the attacker's knifehand with his left forearm, making full use of a twisting hip movement. The defender then steps forward and takes hold of the attacker's wrist with his right hand and strikes the face with a left back fist. *See Figs. 306a and b.* After this, the defender moves forward with his right hand still holding the attacker's wrist, and strikes with his elbow to the face. Immediately he straightens his left arm and forces the attacker's head back. *See Figs. 307a, b, 308a, b.* While he is doing this he must keep pulling the attacker's wrist to the right and holding the attacker's arm under his left arm, twisting the wrist against the joint. *See Figs. 309a and b.*

Fig. 305a

Note 1. The defender holds his own right sleeve with his left hand so that the wrist touches the joint of the attacker's elbow on the outside.

Vote 2. The defender lifts up his wrist on the attacker's elbow joint and twists the wrist of the attacker in a downward movement.

Note 3. The defender must keep his elbow low. *See Fig. 310.*

THE ATTACK WITH A STABBING MOTION

Knife Defence No. 6 (See Figs. 311, 312.)

The attacker hides the knife behind him and suddenly holds it up and stabs at the defender with it. The defender moves his back foot forward to the right, making his body cross in front of the attacker. At the same time he strikes the chin upwards with the heel of his left palm.

Note. When the defender steps forward he must not go to the front of the attacker but to the right, because when the attacker strikes down the defender must be clear of the knife. *See Figs. 311, 312a and b.*

Fig. 305b

Knife Defence No. 7 (See Figs. 313–316.)

This is the same as No. 6, but when the attacker raises his arm to strike, the defender steps forward and blocks with his left forearm in a head block. If the defender's timing is good, the attacker's arm will be broken.

Note. The defender must step forward to the left, so that even if the block is not successful the defender will not be hurt. *See Figs. 313a and b.* The defender can now punch the attacker's armpit with his right middle knuckle fist. *See Figs. 314a and b.* The defender raises his left

continued on page 126

Fig. 306a

Fig. 306b

Fig. 307a

Fig. 307b

Fig. 308a

Fig. 308b

Fig. 309a

Fig. 309b

Fig. 310

Fig. 311

Fig. 312a

Fig. 312b

Fig. 313a

Fig. 313b

Fig. 314a

Fig. 314b

Fig. 315a

Fig. 315b

Fig. 315c

Fig. 316a

Fig. 316b

Fig. 316c

Fig. 317a

Fig. 317b

Fig. 317c

Fig. 318a

Fig. 318b

Fig. 318c

Fig. 319a

Fig. 319b

Fig. 319c

Fig. 320a

Fig. 320b

Fig. 320c

Fig. 321a

Fig. 321b

Fig. 321c

Fig. 322a

Fig. 322b

Fig. 322c

Fig. 323a

Fig. 323b

Fig. 323c

· Fig. 324

Fig. 325a

Fig. 325b

Fig. 326a

Fig. 326b

Fig. 327

Fig. 328

Fig. 329

Fig. 330a

Fig. 330b

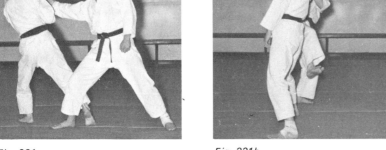

Fig. 331a

Fig. 331b

Fig. 332a

hand, holding the attacker's hand at the back, twists with the inside of his thumb against the root of the attacker's thumb and with his other fingers pushes the attacker's little finger. At the same time the defender opens his right hand and, pushing against the middle of the attacker's upper arm, steps forward on his right foot, twists his left wrist and attacks with a right elbow. *See Figs. 315a, b, c, 316a, b, c.*

Knife Defence No. 8 (*See Figs. 317–323.*)

The attacker steps forward and attacks from the side. The defender avoids this by twisting his body and then, when he is attacked once more, steps forward, holds the attacker's arm and turns behind his body. He then pushes up the attacker's chin with his right hand, and with his left strikes with a knifehand to the ribs. The attacker is now defenceless so the defender grasps his hair and kicks him in the kidneys with his left foot. Pulling back his body quickly to the right, the defender forces the attacker down. As the first attack comes from the right it is important to judge correctly the distance between and then block, twisting the waist from left to right.

Note. If the defender withdraws too much he cannot counter-attack. *See Figs. 317a, b, c, 318a, b, c, 319a, b, c, 320a, b, c, 321a, b, c, 322a, b, c, 323a, b, c.*

Fig. 332b

Knife Defence No. 9 (*See Figs. 324–332.*)

The attacker moves straight forward with the knife held above his head (*Fig. 324*). The defender judges the distance, moves his right foot backwards and to the left. At the same time he leans his body backwards, so avoiding the knife. *See Figs. 325a and b.* The defender holds the attacker's knifehand with his left hand following down the attacker's movement, and kicks with a roundhouse kick. *See Figs. 326a, b, 327, 328, 329, 330a, b, 331a, b, 332a, b.*

Note. Before the defender kicks, he must twist the attacker's hand, to avoid the knife.

11 FREE SPARRING

In free sparring in Karate, as in 'rampo' in Judo and sparring in boxing, the participants fight applying all the usual attacking and blocking techniques learnt in practice, basic sparring and semi-free sparring (all of which have been described in earlier chapters). Free sparring could be said to be the essence of perfect skill in Karate. Therefore, it is not only useless for beginners to practise it, but also dangerous. It is wrong that some beginners practise free sparring without first acquiring the essential basic techniques. As a Japanese proverb says, 'The longest way round is the shortest way home.' If you hurry in training you will not make progress beyond a certain limit, because it is impossible for you to change or apply techniques freely in a given situation without first acquiring many techniques.

It is most regrettable that since Karate contests have become popular recently in Japan, people have tended to use less important techniques. They have acquired these techniques with the sole intention of winning contests, and have neglected such skills as clear focusing, or the art of knocking down the opponent unfailingly with one punch only, both of which are peculiar to Karate. Another reason is the neglect of basic techniques and forms.

Points to Note

1. *To master blocking techniques*
There is a saying, 'Attack is the best method of defence.' But you can only apply this if you have first thoroughly mastered perfect blocking techniques. It is sometimes said that a man with an attacking style is weak in defence, but this is only because he has not mastered the blocking techniques.

Even in continuous attacking there is a limit. Any attacker inevitably becomes short of breath for a few seconds at some time, and there is a slacking off in attack. If you keep on blocking perfectly, the opponent loses patience or relaxes his attention for a moment, and then you can counter-attack and knock him down. But to do this, you must always have the whole of your body full of an attacking spirit, ready for any chance. Do not become occupied solely with your blocking, as I said in the chapter 'What is Karate?'

Mrs. Omatsu, manager of the women's volleyball team in Japan which won a gold medal in the Tokyo Olympic Games, invented their famous receiving techniques, in the belief that 'Perfect defence is the way to victory.' It is perfect defence that those who practise Karate must learn whole-heartedly. In Karate, if your defence is not perfect, you are in real danger of being injured.

2. *A Rational Combination of Blows*
Although Karate is often called the art of knocking down with one blow, what do you do when your fist is blocked by the opponent's perfect

defence? It is possible to block adequately an attack that cannot be avoided, without any harm or damage, just as you can always catch a hard ball without pain by withdrawing your hand as you receive it.

To describe Karate as 'the art of knocking down an enemy unfailingly with one blow', is liable to cause misunderstanding, but what it means is that you must always have the *intention* of knocking down your opponent with one blow. That is to say, these words emphasize a serious, uncompromising attitude in practice. If you fail one such attack, your next attack must follow immediately.

It is important to apply a varied combination of blows, in which the attack develops naturally, almost of its own accord, without losing one's balance, in sequences of attacking techniques. For example, immediately after attacking the head, one could kick at the stomach, or after attacking the knee, one could follow up by striking at the head.

Various techniques are illustrated here as examples, but it is up to you to produce good applied techniques by yourself. Those outlined are just basic techniques.

3. *Body-shift*

Most beginners shift only forward or backwards while attacking or blocking. It is the most essential, and the most difficult, technique in Karate to shift to the right or to the left. You will have very limited opportunity to counter-attack if you withdraw backwards when your opponent is attacking you. If you shift to the right or to the left, however, it is possible to block a strong attack by your opponent, using only the minimum of strength; furthermore, it is possible to counter-attack quickly, as your opponent will remain well within range.

4. *Kiai* (*Mesmerizing*)

Kiai is the art of developing fighting spirit, almost of self-hypnosis, by extreme mental concentration. In order to perform one's attacking or blocking techniques properly, it is necessary to develop perfect concentration of spirit and strength. Only if you concentrate your whole strength in your abdomen and maintain perfect balance, will you achieve the art of aggression and of knocking your opponent down at one blow.

Kind of Kiai

(a) *Kiai without Yelling*

When warding off the opponent's Kiai, you must also put your strength in the abdomen in order to keep up your courage. When the opportunity to attack comes, you must use your Kiai in attacking—i.e. put your strength in your abdomen, and concentrate your whole effort on the punch or kick.

(b) *Kiai with Yelling*

This is the same thing as the Kiai described above, but the difference is that you yell at the same time. In yelling you must yell from the whole of your body, not only from your mouth.

The sounds made in 'Kiai with yelling' are ei, oh, ya, orya, and so on. Ei is the easiest to yell. The object of yelling is to weaken the opponent's attack or to put him off his guard, and so one must yell properly in each given situation. It is important to practise yelling without restraint and at the top of your voice, preferably in a deserted place! It is said that there was once a student of Karate who improved his yelling after hearing a lion roaring in the zoo!

ATTACKING AND BLOCKING TECHNIQUES

All the following techniques are very good for self-defence and can be practised in free fighting, but some kicks and punches, etc., cannot be used in contests because they are considered fouls. For example; sokuto

Fig. 333a

Fig. 333b

Fig. 334a

Fig. 334b

Fig. 335a

Fig. 335b

Fig. 336a

Fig. 336b

Fig. 337

Fig. 338a

Fig. 338b

Fig. 339a

Fig. 339b

Fig. 340a

Fig. 340b

Fig. 341a

Fig. 341b

Fig. 342a

Fig. 342b

Fig. 343a

Fig. 343b

Fig. 344a

Fig. 344b

Fig. 345a

fumikome (foot edge knee kick). Some of the Ohyo Gumite techniques are similar to free fighting, so it is possible to select techniques and make up combinations for free fighting. These techniques are basic and during free fighting it may be necessary to alter or adapt them slightly. The photographs show one side only. The techniques must, however, be practised both from the left and right positions.

Hand Attacking Techniques

(1) *See Figs. 333a, b, 334a, b, 335a, b.*
Both in left front stance. A moves forwards as shown and attacks to the face with a back fist. B blocks. A does not pull the fist back but follows through, opening the hands slightly into palm heel. He then twists his hips to the right and brings up the palm heel and strikes B under the chin.

Note 1. The body must be relaxed all the time except when striking with the back fist and palm heel. All combination techniques must be correct, very quick, and be made without stopping.

Note 2. The back fist attack must be delivered strongly in order that the following palm heel strike will be effective.

(2) *See Figs. 336a, b, 337, 338a, b, 339a, b, 340a, b, 341a, b.*
A is in right stance, B is in left stance. A brings up his left foot into left stance and at the same time the hips are twisted quickly to the right and the weight of the body moves forward. The attack is made either up B's chin with the left palm heel or the clawhand to the neck. A then turns quickly 180° to the right and strikes the face with an elbow attack if B is very near, or, if B is further away with a back fist or knifehand attack to the neck.

Note. During the 180° turn the knees must be bent to maintain a good balance.

(3) *See Figs. 342a, b, 343a, b, 344a, b.*
A is in left stance, B is in right stance. A moves both feet forward, then with a left knifehand he pushes B's arms slightly. He then attacks B's face with a swing striking with a right reverse fist.

(4) *See Figs. 345a, b, 346a, b, 347a, b.*
A is in left stance, B is in right stance. A moves both feet forward and feints with his right hand to B's face. B lifts his arms up to guard his face, then A pulls back his right arm in an arc and strikes B in the stomach with a ridgehand.

(5) *See Figs. 348, 349, 350.*
A is in left stance, B is in right stance. A moves forward and punches to B's face with left hand, then punches in a sideways arc to B's stomach with a ridgehand.

(6) *See Figs. 351, 352, 353.*
Both are in left stance. A moves forward, stamping on B's left foot with his left foot. At the same time he grabs B's left wrist with his left hand and pushes strongly. Then A punches with right reverse punch to the side ribs.

Blocking and Counter Punching against Attacks to the Head

(1) *See Figs. 354, 355a, b, 356a, b, 357a, b, 358a, b.*
A is in right stance and B is in left stance. A steps forward slightly with his right foot and punches to B's face with his right hand. B side-steps slightly to the left and at the same time twists his hips to the right, bringing up his arm a little and blocking with his left forearm. This block is done before A's arms straightens, then, as A's arm completes the punch, B straightens his arm and twists in a clockwise motion. This defence is block and counter-punch simultaneously:

continued on page 134

Fig. 345b

Fig. 346a

Fig. 346b

Fig. 347a

Fig. 347b

Fig. 348

Fig. 349

Fig. 350

Fig. 351

Fig. 352

Fig. 353

Fig. 354

Fig. 355a

Fig. 355b

Fig. 356a

Fig. 356b

Fig. 357a

Fig. 357b

Fig. 358a

Fig. 358b

Fig. 359a

Fig. 359b

Fig. 360a

Fig. 360b

(2) *See Figs. 359a and b.*
A is in right stance, B is in left stance. A steps forwards with right foot and punches with his right hand to B's face. B takes his right foot back slightly and sways back with the other part of the body. At the same time he raises his left arm up, blocking the punch. This block is delivered with the arm bent and the fist strikes the attacker's face at the same time.

(3) *See Figs. 360a, b, 361a, b, 362a, b.*
Both are in left stance. A punches at the face with his left hand. B moves his right foot to the left and leans his head back. With his open right hand he blocks A's punch. This block is delivered with the back of the hand, keeping the elbow in to the body and snapping the wrist. Simultaneously, the left hand punches upwards under A's chin. B then steps sideways with the left foot and punches A's ribs with the right elbow punch.

Note. The hips must be twisted quickly to the right, both knees must be bent and the body must lean backwards away from the punch.

(4) *See Figs. 363a, b, 364a, b, 365a, b, 366a, b.*
A is left stance, B is right stance. A punches to the face with his left hand. B steps back slightly with his foot and sways back with his upper body. At the same time he twists his hips to the left and swings up his right elbow, blocking A's punch. With a continuous movement he counterpunches to A's stomach with his back fist. He then twists his hips to the right and punches with his ridgehand to A's groin.

(5) *See Figs. 367a, b, c, 368a, b, c, 369a, b, c, 370a, b, c, 371a, b, c, 372a, b, c.*
Both are in right stance. A punches to the face with his right hand. B moves back slightly, opens his right hand and with an up and down hooking movement, blocks the punch to the right with the back of his right hand. At the same time he twists his hips quickly to the right. Also, the left hand moves up, comes down in an arc and grips A's forearm, forcing it downwards. B then strikes the side of A's chin with an upward movement of his right elbow. At the same time B's right foot moves forward with the elbow strike. B grips A's collar with his right hand, pushing him down, and at the same time brings up his knee quickly to strike A in the stomach. This is followed by a downward elbow strike to the back of A's neck. B's right foot must be stamped quickly to the floor to add speed to the elbow strike.

(6) *See Figs. 373a and b.*
Any stance. A punches to the face. B does not move the feet but sways his upper body away from the attack. At the same time he kicks with his front foot to the stomach. This technique needs very good timing.

(7) *See Fig. 374.*
Both are in left stance. A punches to B's face with his left hand. B sways back with his upper body and kicks to A's groin with the instep of his front foot. Good timing is essential.

(8) *See Figs. 375, 376, 377.*
Both are in left stance. A attacks to the face with his left hand. B moves his left foot across the right foot and backward, at the same time bending his body forward and twisting his hips to the right. He then counterkicks to A's stomach with a back kick. Good timing and good judge of distance are essential.

(9) *See Figs. 378a, b, c, 379a, b, c, 380a, b, 381a, b, c.*
A is in right stance, B left stance. A attacks to B's face. B lifts his front foot and counter-kicks to A's knee with a foot edge stamp kick. B then moves his left foot slightly to the left and kicks to A's face or stomach with a roundhouse kick.

continued on page 140

Fig. 361a

Fig. 361b

Fig. 362a

Fig. 362b

Fig. 363a

Fig. 363b

Fig. 364a

Fig. 364b

Fig. 365a

Fig. 365b

Fig. 366a

Fig. 366b

Fig. 367a

Fig. 367b

Fig. 367c

Fig. 368a

Fig. 368b

Fig. 368c

Fig. 369a

Fig. 369b

Fig. 369c

Fig. 370a

Fig. 370b

Fig. 370c

Fig. 371a

Fig. 371b

Fig. 371c

Fig. 372a

Fig. 372b

Fig. 372c

Fig. 373a

Fig. 373b

Fig. 374

Fig. 375

Fig. 376

Fig. 377

Fig. 378a

Fig. 378b

Fig. 378c

Fig. 379a

Fig. 379b

Fig. 379c

Fig. 380a

Fig. 380b

Fig. 381a

Fig. 381b

Fig. 381c

Fig. 382

Fig. 383

Fig. 385a

Fig. 385b

Fig. 384

Fig. 386a

Fig. 386b

(10) *See Figs. 382, 383, 384.*
Any stance. A attacks to the face. B then counter-kicks to the ribs under A's arm with a foot edge kick delivered with the front foot. Good timing and speed are essential.

Blocking and Counter Punch against Attack to the Body

(1) *See Figs. 385a, b, 386a, b, 387a, b.*
A is in left stance and B right stance. A attacks the body with his left hand. B brings his front foot up to the back one, pulling back his lower body. Twisting slightly with his hips to the left he lifts his left hand up with the hand open. Then he brings it down in an arc and blocks the attacking punch with the palm of his hand. At the same time the right hand moves in to the body, then goes forward in an arc and strikes A's face with the back fist.

(2) *See Figs. 388a, b, c, 389a, b, c, 390a, b, c.*
A is in left stance, B is in right stance. A attacks B's body with his left hand. B moves his left leg to the left and his right hand moves up slightly, then down and back, blocking the punch with the back elbow in one continuous movement. The right hand then moves forward, striking A's chin.

Attacking with the foot

(1) *See Figs. 391, 392.*
A is in left stance, B right stance. A attacks the groin with a light kick from the back foot and B blocks with crossed hands. A pulls back his foot a little and immediately attacks the face with a roundhouse kick, twisting his hips at the same time. The first kick must be light and the roundhouse kick strong. Both kicks must be very quickly delivered.

(2) *See Figs. 393, 394.*
Both are in left stance. B moves the back foot up to the front and sways the body slightly back. At the same time he kicks to the groin with a roundhouse kick, using the instep.

(3) *See Figs. 395a, b, 396a, b, 397a, b.*
Both are in right stance. B sweeps A's right foot with the sole of his left foot, the foot moving in an arc. Moving the left foot slightly to the left, he then kicks to A's stomach and face with a right roundhouse kick.

(4) *See Figs. 398a, b, 399a, b, 400a, b, 401a, b.*
Both are in left stance, but standing a little further away than usual. B steps forward with his right leg and twist his hips to the left. This movement must be done very quickly and with body relaxed. Turn the right foot to the right and kick with a left roundhouse kick to the stomach.

(5) *See Figs. 402, 403, 404, 405.*
B is in left stance and A right stance. With his left foot B kicks with a one step front kick, but the kick is only a weak one. Then, placing the left foot down slightly more to the left, he kicks with a strong roundhouse kick.

(6) *See Figs. 406a, b, 407a, b, 408a, b, 409, 410.*
Both are in left stance. B kicks with a one step foot edge stamping knee kick. A pulls back his left foot away from the kick. After the kick, B puts his foot down to the right, turns 180° to the right and kicks with a back kick to the stomach. When the kick is completed, B again turns 180° to the right, facing front once more, and strikes with either a back fist to the face or a reverse punch to the stomach.

Note 1. It is important to have the correct distance for the back kick so, if the distance is too short, move the left foot back slightly; if too long, then move the left foot forward slightly.

continued on page 145

Fig. 387a

Fig. 387b

Fig. 388a

Fig. 388b

Fig. 388c

Fig. 389a

Fig. 389b

Fig. 389c

Fig. 390a

Fig. 390b

Fig. 390c

Fig. 391

Fig. 392

Fig. 393

Fig. 394

Fig. 395a

Fig. 395b

Fig. 396a

Fig. 396b

Fig. 397a

Fig. 397b

Fig. 398a

Fig. 398b

Fig. 399a

Fig. 399b

Fig. 400a

Fig. 400b

Fig. 401a

Fig. 401b

Fig. 402

Fig. 403

Fig. 404

Fig. 405

Fig. 406a

Fig. 406b

Fig. 407a

143

Fig. 407b

Fig. 408a

Fig. 408b

Fig. 409

Fig. 410

Fig. 411a

Fig. 411b

Fig. 411c

Fig. 412a

Fig. 412b

Fig. 412c

Fig. 413a

Note 2. On both the turns it is important to maintain a good balance.

(7) *See Figs. 411a, b, c, 412a, b, c, 413a, b, 414a, b.*
A is in right stance and B left stance. B leans his body forward slightly and grasps A's sleeve with his right hand. He moves his right foot up to his left foot and simultaneously pulls with his right hand and stamp kicks at A's right knee with a left foot edge kick. B follows up by jumping in with a scissors movement, his left leg up and his right leg low behind A's leg. Twisting to the left, he brings A to the ground. After throwing, B attacks the face with his right hand.

(8) *See Figs. 415, 416, 417.*
A is in left stance and B in right stance. B kicks to A's stomach with a roundhouse kick. A moves back slightly without changing his stance. After the kick, B turns, kicks with a back kick and attacks as in No. 6 above.

(9) *See Figs. 418, 419, 420.*
Any stance. B feints to the face with a back fist, lifting his body at the same time. He then quickly leans his body to the left and kicks to A's body with a foot edge kick.

Blocking Techniques against a Kick

The Front kick Block

(1) *See Figs. 421a, b, c.*
Both are in same stance. From the left stance A kicks with a front kick with the back foot. B moves his left foot to the left and twists his hips to the right. Making full use of the twist, either by opening his left hand or with his fist, he blocks the kick from left to right, in a sweeping movement. The position, when he blocks, should be : Weight on rear foot—hips lowered and body upright. His right fist should be at the ready position on his right hip. As soon as the block is completed a strike is made to the ribs or face using the ridgehand, elbow, reverse punch, or roundhouse kick. *See Figs. 422, 423, 424, 425.*

(2) *See Figs. 426, 427a, b, 428, 429a, b.*
Both are in same stance. When A slides forward half a step, B moves his front foot backward half a step. The block and strike are the same as in No. 1.

(3) *See Figs. 430, 431a, b, 432a, b.*
Both are in same stance. With the left stance A slides forward half a step and kicks front kick. B withdraws obliquely to the right using the left foot, then the right foot. With the hips twisted to the right, B turns his left hand and blocks to the left. It is important to move the body sufficiently sideways and twist to the right, when blocking.

(4) *See Figs. 433, 434a, b, 435.*
When the stances are reversed, A kicks front kick with his right back foot. B then withdraws to the left as in No. 3, blocks and attacks.

(5) *See Figs. 436a, b.*
Both are in same stance as soon as A kicks with his back foot, B steps forward with his front foot and takes a pace with his back foot. Blocking the kick to the side with his leading forearm, B then strikes a reverse punch to the stomach before A's blocked kick reaches its extremity. Speed and good timing are therefore essential.

(6) *See Figs. 437a, b, c.*
Both are in opposite stance. When A uses his rear foot to deliver a front kick, B moves his back foot slightly sideways and his front foot straight forward, blocking with his left arm. With his body leaning forward, B punches at A's stomach with a one knuckle fist. It is very important to

continued on page 150

Fig. 413b

Fig. 414a

Fig. 414b

Fig. 415

Fig. 416

Fig. 417

Fig. 418

Fig. 419

Fig. 420

Fig. 421a

Fig. 421b

Fig. 421c

Fig. 422

Fig. 423

Fig. 424

Fig. 425

Fig. 426

Fig. 427a

Fig. 427b

Fig. 428

Fig. 429a

Fig. 429b

Fig. 430

Fig. 431a

Fig. 431b

Fig. 432a

Fig. 432b

Fig. 433

Fig. 434a

Fig. 434b

Fig. 435

Fig. 436a

Fig. 436b

Fig. 437a

Fig. 437b

Fig. 437c

Fig. 438a

Fig. 438b

Fig. 439

Fig. 440

Fig. 441

develop good timing and twisting technique to avoid the kick. Moving forward and back as necessary.

(7) *See Figs. 438a, b.*
B should bring his knee up to cover the groin, when blocking a front kick that is low.

The Way to Block a Roundhouse Kick

(1) *See Fig. 439.*
Blocking a good roundhouse kick by using the hand or arm is difficult, therefore it is necessary to move forward towards the kick to reduce its effectiveness or make it miss.

(2) *See Figs. 440, 441.*
A is in left stance, B in right stance. A delivers a roundhouse kick to the stomach and B moves back into the opposite stance taking the kick on the shoulder near the top of the arm.

12 KARATE CONTESTS

Contests Today

The present-day match rules were established by the All-Japan Karate Association (Wado school) in June 1957, and the first Karate match, with teams from fourteen universities competing, was held at the gymnasium of Meiji University in Tokyo in the same year.

This was the first time in the history of Karate that it was organized as a sport with matches. The rules applied on that occasion have been adopted in Japan and in every country in the world where Karate is practised today.

The main principle underlying these rules is that a blow must be stopped before it reaches the opponent. Actual striking is prohibited as a foul. To avoid injury beginners are not allowed to take part in matches in Japan. This is very necessary. As time goes by, Karate will become more and more popular, and matches will be held more and more frequently, and so it is essential that leaders of Karate should not allow beginners to take part in contests.

Contest Technique

The techniques used in contests are somewhat different at present from those adopted for free sparring. Since in contests it is forbidden to actually strike, punch, or kick an opponent, each contestant must stop his blow before it actually makes contact. In free sparring, of course, the object is actually to strike one's opponent. If a contestant were to stop his blow before it reached his opponent, his Karate might well lose its sense of purpose. Neither could it be ascertained whether or not the blow would have reached its target. Therefore in free sparring we expect blows, for example to the face, with the open hand, so that the opponent can block spiritedly, and learn to develop his next attack out of the blocking movement.

In present-day contests, however, actual striking is a foul, and so if you are struck in the face, you become the winner, by a 'foul win'.

It is very unfortunate that for this reason there is nowadays a tendency in matches to block without any real spirit. This is against the spirit of Karate, and we ought to take steps to prevent it. One point is that some of the present rules governing matches could be improved. For example, some kind of protector could be used and the 'foul win' abolished. However, it is difficult to envisage a protector which would still enable one to use all the techniques which are unique in Karate. Nevertheless, some such device is clearly needed, perhaps along the lines of the protector in Japanese fencing matches, in which a small light lights up when the edge of the sword touches the fencer.

Preparation for a Contest

1. *Preparing One's Mind*

In Japan, the samurai who used to fight in single combat on the battlefield had a saying learned in training: 'Daunted on hearing; cowed at sight; inadequacy in training.'

This means that if you are daunted at hearing your opponent's reputation, or if you are cowed when you see your opponent's fearless look of his great strength you will be defeated, but if you are defeated without being daunted on hearing or cowed at sight, it is because of some inadequacy in your training. If you train yourself keeping these three precepts in your mind, it is said that you will not be defeated.

2. Tactics

You must keep your eyes on those of your opponent while making the bow. If you find your opponent is unguarded at the call of Hajime (start), that is, if his eyes are not on you, thrust yourself forward and attack him. It is a good chance to win. If, however, you see that your opponent is about to rush into the attack full of fighting spirit, step forward one step and attack him, or else shift sideways abruptly and attack him quickly at the moment when he is startled. These tactics of the first movement are very important.

Secondly, study your opponent's good and bad points and try to frustrate him in his intentions. For instance, prepare your stance so that you are not caught by his favourite techniques.

If your opponent is good at hidari mawashigeri (the left roundhouse kick), you must take up the right stance; if his speciality is migimaegeri (the right front kick), you should pretend to withdraw, then step in abruptly and punch with chudanzuki (the stomach punch), or you invite his kick, then block it and punch with gyakuzuki (the reverse punch).

CONTEST RULES

(1) **Contest Officials**

The officials are one referee and four judges. There are also two time-keepers, one announcer, and one recorder.

(2) **Rules for the Guidance of Officials**

(a) *The Referee*
The referee shall be free to move anywhere within the contest area. The referee is in complete control of the contest; he declares *ippongachi* (one point win), explains how the point is scored if necessary, and declares *hansokumake* (lost by foul), and *shikkakumake* (lost by disqualification). He gives any warnings before or during the contest, and any other necessary orders such as any breaks in the contest or any withdrawals, etc. The referee can consult with the judges or seek their advice. For *hantei* (a decision) the referee can award two points. He also declares the result and then the extension of contest time.

(b) *The Judges*
The judges shall be provided with a red and a white flag and a whistle. They shall assist the referee from each corner of the contest area. They shall advise the referee on his decision and also advise him on *ippon* or a foul by blowing a whistle. They will signify by raising a flag for a decision. Each judge can award one point.

(c) *The Controller*
There is one controller who observes the course of the contest and notes the decision of the referee.

(d) *Objection to a Decision*
Only the man who takes the responsibility for each team (team manager) can object to a decision. Objections must be addressed to the controller.

Fig. 442a

Fig. 442b

Fig. 443a

Fig. 443b

Fig. 444

Fig. 445

Fig. 446

Fig. 447

Fig. 448

Fig. 449

Fig. 450

Fig. 451

Fig. 452

Fig. 453

Fig. 454

Fig. 455

Fig. 456

Fig. 457

Fig. 458a

Fig. 458b

The controller after examining the protest, hears the referee's explanation and can ask the referee for another decision.

(3) Rules for Contest

(a) Team Contest
A team shall consist of five contestants. The team with the greater number of winning contestants is declared winner.

(b) Contest Officials and Controller
The contest officials consist of one referee and four judges. The referee is in complete control of the contest. There is also one controller who ensures fair judgement.

(c) Length of Contest
The contest shall last for two minutes from the call *hajime* (begin) by the referee and extra time shall be allowed for any accidents or a conference of contest officials.

(d) Result
The result shall be determined by *ippon* (one point), *hanteigatchi* (win by decision), *hansoku make* (lost by foul), or *shikkaku make* (lost by disqualification).

(e) Ippon, Wazaari (half point), and Yuseigachi (superiority–inferiority)

(i) *Ippon shall be decided by any of the following:*
See Figs. 442a, b, 443a, b, 444, 445, 446, 447.
A. Attack with good karate techniques.
   A correct distance during counter-attack.
   An effective focused punch on the opponent's vital parts.
B. Any other techniques which are recognized scoring techniques, such as counter-attack or a focused punch after throwing.
C. When there are two half point techniques.

(ii) *Wazaari (half point)*
See Figs. 448, 449, 450.
Wazaari can be awarded for a well-timed punch which is slightly off centre, a good punch which is weak or a punch slightly off target but with the opponent unguarded.

(iii) *No Score*
See Figs. 451, 452, 453.
As shown in Fig. 3, throwing alone is no use. A throw must be followed by a strong punch or kick to score. The person thrown must try to block the following punch or kick.

(iv) *Yusei (superiority)* (*Yuseigachi is equal to a half point score*)
When neither contestant has succeeded in scoring or when there is no loss by foul or disqualification during the contest time, the decision of superiority by the referee and judges who will consider the following points;

   (*a*) When there is a half point.
   (*b*) Skilful technique, fighting spirit, or correct attitude.

(v) *Hansoku (foul and disqualification)*
See Figs. 454, 455, 456, 457, 458a and b.

(a) *If a contestant commits a foul, he is declared* hansoku make (*loss by foul*). *The following are fouls:*
A. Actually hitting an opponent's vital parts, except hands and feet, even if it is unintentional.
B. Slapping the face.
C. Attempting to strike the opponent's eye with a spearhand.
D. Performing dangerous throwing techniques.

(b) *Shikkaku. The contestant shall be immediately disqualified and declared the loser as follows:*

A. When he ignores contest rules.

B. If he shows unsportsmanlike behaviour.

C. If one contestant is injured during the contest accidentally or can't continue for other reasons except a foul.

(vi) *Fusen* (*Default*)

(*a*) If one contestant arrives too late for the contest.

(*b*) If one contestant is injured before the contest and can't take part, his opponent is awarded 'winner'.

(4) Equipment

(*a*) Titles and placarding.

(*b*) Microphone.

(*c*) First-aid kit.

(*d*) Forty metres of white tape (131 ft.).

(*e*) Four red and white flags.

(*f*) Six whistles.

(*g*) Seven red belts (about three centimetres (1 in.) wide for contestants).

(*h*) One stop-watch.

(*i*) One bell.

(*j*) Desks and chairs (for contest officials).

(*k*) Two mats.

(*l*) Two scoreboards.

(*m*) Paper for records.

(5) The Method of Recording

(*a*) The names of the two teams, contestants, contest area (A–1 or B–2, etc.) and contest officials are written.

(*b*) The decision of the referee is written in the column for decision.

(*c*) The decisions are marked as follows: O for a win, X for a loss, and ▲ for a draw in the column for result. At the end, write the number of O (wins) in the column for points.

(*d*) Write a small Ⓟ in the column for points when one team scores more *ippongachi* (one point win) when there is a tie.

(*e*) Write a small Ⓣ in the column for points when a chosen member wins the deciding match.

(*f*) After the contest the record of the result is shown to the referee and presented to headquarters after the declaration of the results by the referee.

(*g*) Decision.

Ippongachi (one point win).

Foul win.

Disqualification win.

Default.

Superiority win (decision).

One point for two half points.

(6) A Decision Under the Ranking of the Teams

(*a*) When both teams win the same number of points and also the same number of *ippongachi*, a deciding match shall be played.

(*b*) *Ippongachi* consists of the following:

O one point win

Ⓕ foul win

Ⓓ disqualification win

ⒹⒻ default

(*c*) For a deciding match a member shall be selected from each team (including substitutes).

continued on page 159

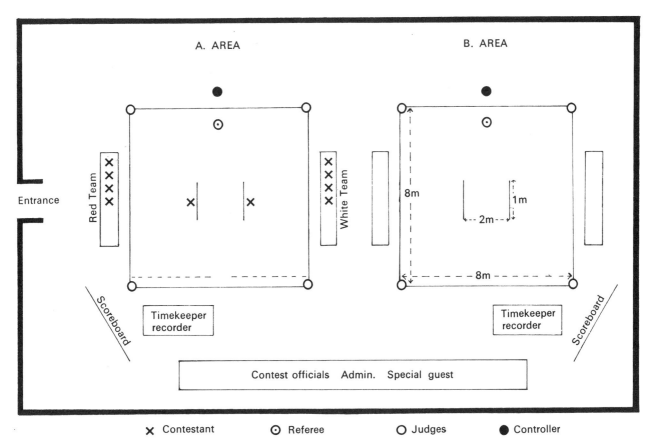

Diag. 81. **Layout of Karate Contest Area**

Area		Ref		Name		Judge	1 2 3 4	
		Controller		Name				
Point		Result						
Red Team		No.	1	2	3	4	5	
		Name						
		Hantei						
		Name						
White Team			1	2	3	4	5	
Point		Result						

Diag. 82. **Record Forms**

157

MARK for RESULT	MARK for HANTEI	EXPLANATION
O Kachi (win)	O	ippongachi (one point winner)
	Ⓕ	hansokugachi (foul win)
	Ⓓ	shikkakugachi (disqualification win)
	ⒹⒻ	fusengachi (default)
	△S̲	vuseigachi (superiority)
	△ △	two half points/Full score
	△	wazaari (half point)
	△ O	wazaari/ippon (half point/one point)
	△ F	wazaari/hansoku (half point/Foul)
▲		hikiwake (draw)
✕		make (lose)

Diag. 83.   The Marks Used to Indicate a Decision

(*d*) When the result cannot be decided by a deciding match, the contest can be extended.

(*e*) When it is necessary to decide the rank, such as in league matches when there are teams level on points, the team which wins the greatest number of *ippongachi* shall be ranked higher. If necessary a conference of test officials can be held. A deciding match is usual in tournament play.

(7) Special Contests and Results

(*a*) In eliminations the team with the last winner is declared winner.

(*b*) When the number of regular team members is insufficient for the contest, the team shall be disqualified.

(*c*) When an injury occurs during the contest and the contest cannot be continued :

(i) when neither contestants has succeeded in scoring the result will be determined by a conference of referee and judges, and by seeking the advice of the controller ;

(ii) when one contestant has won a half point. Unless the injury is made by a foul, the contestant with the half point shall be recognized as the winner.

(*d*) When a contestant who does not belong to the team takes part in the contest, the team shall be disqualified.

(8) The Method of Timing the Contest

The contest shall continue for two minutes from the call *shobuhajime* (start) and it is timed by a stop-watch. After one and a half minutes, the first bell shall be rung, which indicates that there are 30 seconds left. After the two minutes (when time is up) the second bell shall be rung. However, when the referee declares 'wait' to the timekeeper, the time of waiting is added on to the end of the contest.

A deciding match shall be of two minutes' duration and extra time usually one minute. (In extra time the first bell '30 seconds to go' shall not be rung.)

(9) Etiquette

(*a*) Before and after a contest, the referee, with the judges on both sides, stands outside the contest area facing the front. Contestants of both teams stand in a line, facing each other, outside the area. All of them make a bow to the front at the order of the programme director. Contestants bow to the referee and judges and after that both teams bow to each other. Then the contestants sit down.

(*b*) The contestants indicated by the referee come to the area, bow to each other and wait for the referee's call *hajime* (start).

(*c*) After the referee's call *soremade* (stop) his decision is made and the contestants bow to each other, withdraw, and sit down.

(*d*) Both contestants shall sit (*seiza*) while either of them adjusts his *karategi*.

(*e*) Bandages can be used during the contest.

(10) Commands of the Referee

(*a*) *Shobu ippon hajime* (start the match).

(*b*) *Yame* (stop) *Jyogai* (outside the area) *Chuoni modoru* (go back to the centre).

(*c*) *Tsuzukete Hajime* (start again after the contestants come back to the centre of the contest area).

(*d*) *Wazaari* (half point) or *Ippon* (one point). When they come back to their starting position the referee indicates the point on the body that was effectively attacked.

(*e*) *Soremade* or *Yame* (stop). When time is up.

(*f*) *Hantei* (A decision). The referee, standing outside the area in the centre of the rear line (where he can see all the flags of the judges) whistles to ask the judges to show flags for *hantei*, and then he determines *hantei*. Returning to his position he declares his decision.

An example of the declaration of *Hansoku* (A foul): 'Rising punch by white is a foul. Therefore red wins.'

(11) Rules for the Referee

(*a*) The referee shall examine contestant's injury before a contest and adjust karategi.

(*b*) The same as above during contest.

(*c*) Contestants shall not wear glasses during a contest.

(*d*) The referee shall be ready to stop a contest whenever contestants get so excited as to be dangerous.

(*e*) When this occurs the referee stops the contest, returns the contestants to the centre, gives a warning to them and then allows the contest to continue.

(*f*) The referee will respect the judges' decision, but he alone is in control of the contest.

(*g*) When the referee declares half point he shall lower his hand downwards to the side of the half point winner, and when he declares one point he shall raise his hands to the winner's side.

(12) Rules for Judges

(*a*) The judges shall advise the referee by watching scoring techniques and any fouls, etc., from their position.

(*b*) The judges, by raising their flags, can advise the referee on a decision if his vision is obscured.

(*c*) The judges shall hold the red flag in their right hand, and the white flag in their left hand.

(*d*) The judges shall wave the flag downward several times for no score and they shall raise their red or white flags for a scoring point.

(*e*) When the referee whistles, each judge will indicate his decision by raising a red or white flag (when they decide on a draw, they will cross their flags above their heads).

(13) Rules for the Guidance of the Controller

(*a*) The Controller can accept the team manager's objection and he can ask the referee to make another decision.

(*b*) The Controller will observe the course of the contest and if he sees anything wrong he will call the referee by blowing his whistle and ask him to put it right. He shall do the same to the judges.

(14) Others

(*a*) Any conference between the referee and the judges must be of short duration.

(*b*) The referee, when he announces a decision, should speak briefly and clearly.